CENTRE FOR EDUCATIONAL RESEARCH AND INNOVATION

HUMAN CAPITAL INVESTMENT

An International Comparison

ORGANISATION FOR ECONOMIC CO-OPERATION AND DEVELOPMENT

BL T 5924-3/2

ORGANISATION FOR ECONOMIC CO-OPERATION AND DEVELOPMENT

Pursuant to Article 1 of the Convention signed in Paris on 14th December 1960, and which came into force th September 1961, the Organisation for Economic Co-operation and Development (OECD) shall promote es designed:

- to achieve the highest sustainable economic growth and employment and a rising standard of living in Member countries, while maintaining financial stability, and thus to contribute to the development of the world economy;
- to contribute to sound economic expansion in Member as well as non-member countries in the process of economic development; and
- to contribute to the expansion of world trade on a multilateral, non-discriminatory basis in accordance with international obligations.

The original Member countries of the OECD are Austria, Belgium, Canada, Denmark, France, Germany, Greece, Iceland, Ireland, Italy, Luxembourg, the Netherlands, Norway, Portugal, Spain, Sweden, Switzerland, Turkey, the United Kingdom and the United States. The following countries became Members subsequently through accession at the dates indicated hereafter: Japan (28th April 1964), Finland (28th January 1969), Australia (7th June 1971), New Zealand (29th May 1973), Mexico (18th May 1994), the Czech Republic (21st December 1995), Hungary (7th May 1996), Poland (22nd November 1996) and Korea (12th December 1996). The Commission of the European Communities takes part in the work of the OECD (Article 13 of the OECD Convention).

The Centre for Educational Research and Innovation was created in June 1968 by the Council of the Organisation for Economic Co-operation and Development and all Member countries of the OECD are participants.

The main objectives of the Centre are as follows:

- *analyse and develop research, innovation and key indicators in current and emerging education and learning issues, and their links to other sectors of policy;*
- *explore forward-looking coherent approaches to education and learning in the context of national and international cultural, social and economic change; and*
- *facilitate practical co-operation among Member countries and, where relevant, with non-member countries, in order to seek solutions and exchange views of educational problems of common interest.*

The Centre functions within the Organisation for Economic Co-operation and Development in accordance with the decisions of the Council of the Organisation, under the authority of the Secretary-General. It is supervised by a Governing Board composed of one national expert in its field of competence from each of the countries participating in its programme of work.

Publié en français sous le titre :
L'INVESTISSEMENT DANS LE CAPITAL HUMAIN
Une comparaison internationale

Photo Credit: PIX/Geoff Brightling

FOREWORD

Knowledge, skills and competences constitute a vital asset in supporting economic growth and reducing social inequality in OECD countries. This asset, which is often referred to as human capital, has been identified as one key factor in combating high and persistent unemployment and the problems of low pay and poverty. As we move into "knowledge-based" economies the importance of human capital becomes even more significant than ever.

Against a background of tight fiscal constraints in almost all countries, Governments are concerned about the importance of measuring the impact of education and training budgets on economic performance and the welfare of societies. Together with businesses and individuals, public authorities share a common interest in renewing and increasing the skills base of the population and workforce. Moreover, there is an increased awareness of the importance of lifelong learning in a society where economic, social and technological change call for flexibility, adaptation and learning throughout life. These were some of the principal considerations which prompted Ministers meeting in the Council of the OECD in 1996 to request the OECD "to develop an initial set of indicators of human capital investment based on existing data, analyse areas where significant gaps remain in internationally comparable data, identify the cost of development of data collection for new measures and performance indicators". This report is a response to that request.

Drawing on a range of indicators based on existing data, the report also highlights key policy-related issues such as the important role of both private and public agents in sponsoring and funding learning throughout life, as well as inequality in access to training by different groups. An important conclusion is that it is insufficient to rely upon aggregate measures of the amount of human capital. It is also important to know how human capital is distributed among different groups in the population, as well as how skills and knowledge are employed in everyday life.

While the report focuses on information and data from existing sources, it also identifies key areas in which new information about human capital investment is needed to guide policy-making. These relate to areas which include workplace learning and skills, as well as the need for measures of a broader range of skills. It is vital to know more about how investments of time and money in human capital yield social and economic benefits, and what types of human capital investment yield the greatest returns. Many of these benefits go far beyond additional employment or earnings for individuals. They relate to the political and social cohesion of OECD Member countries. This report demonstrates that we have still far to go in addressing many of these information needs.

Donald J. Johnston
Secretary-General of the OECD

ACKNOWLEDGMENTS

This report results from a collective effort by members of the Centre for Educational Resarch and Innovation at the OECD including Tom Healy who was principally responsible, and David Istance. The report was also prepared with the assistance of Donald Hirsch, an international policy consultant, Philip O'Connell, of the Economic and Social Research Institute, Ireland and Vincent Vandenberghe, of the Catholic University of Louvain-la-Neuve. The report benefited from the comments and observations made on earlier drafts of this report by various staff members of the Directorate for Education, Employment, Labour and Social Affairs, the Directorate for Science, Technology and Industry, the Economic Department and the Statistics Directorate of OECD as well as members of the Employment, Labour and Social affairs Committee, Education Committee, Governing Board of the Centre for Educational Resarch and Innovation and participants in a meeting of experts in March 1997.

This report is published on the responsibility of the Secretary-General of the OECD.

TABLE OF CONTENTS

Chapter 1.   **The Importance, Scope and Measurement of Human Capital**

1. Growing interest in human capital 7
2. The strategic role of human capital investment 8
3. Defining the scope of human capital 9
4. Analysis and measures 10
References 13

Chapter 2.   **Measuring the Stock of Human Capital**

1. Three approaches to measuring human capital stock 15
2. Measuring educational attainment 16
3. Measuring adult skills directly 22
4. Estimating the market value of human capital 28
5. Beyond individual characteristics 29
6. Conclusions 30
References 34

Chapter 3.   **Investment in Human Capital**

1. Measuring the resources invested 35
2. Financial measures of investment 36
3. Time investment: measuring participation 42
4. Conclusions 48
References 51

Chapter 4.   **Returns to Investment in Human Capital**

1. Benefits, costs and returns 53
2. Evidence of benefits of investment in human capital 54
3. Calculating rates of return 68
4. Conclusions 73
References 76

Chapter 5.   **Improving the Knowledge Base: Indicators, Data and Research Needs**

1. Identifying the principal gaps 81
2. From measuring participation in education and training to measuring human capital 82
3. Comparing investment costs with benefits 84
4. The cost of data collection 88
5. Conclusion: balancing measurement and understanding 89
References 90

Chapter 6.   **Human Capital Investment: Policy Issues and Questions**

1. The policy context 91
2. Five policy issues 92

Annex: Data for the figures 97

LIST OF FIGURES

2.1. Two measures of educational attainment of the adult population 17
2.2. Percentage of younger (25-34 year olds) and older adults (45-54) with upper secondary education
      or higher, 1995 19
2.3. Adults performing above and below an adequate threshold of literacy, 1994-95 25
2.4. Literacy levels of workers in different economic sectors 26
2.5. Adult literacy and educational attainment 27
3.1. Spending on education relative to national income, 1994 37
3.2. Average expected years of formal education, 1995 43
3.3. Percentage participation of employed adults (aged 25-64) in job-related training, 1994-95 45
3.4. Average duration of job-related training undertaken by employed adults aged 25-64, 1994-95 ... 47
4.1A. Percentage of women aged 30-44 in employment, by level of educational attainment, 1995 55
4.1B. Expected years of unemployment over a working lifetime, by level of educational attainment
      for men aged 25-64, 1995 56
4.2. Education and earnings of persons aged 30-44, 1995 58
4.3. Costs and benefits of human capital investment 69
4.4. Annual rates of return to education 71

LIST OF TABLES

2.1. Number of research and development employees per 10 000 individuals
      in the labour force, 1994 30
3.1. Public expenditures on labour market training programmes in OECD countries, 1995 39
3.2. Expenditure on vocational training as a percentage of total labour costs 40
3.3. Participation in continuing education and training by adults:
      summary of results from the *International Adult Literacy Survey* in 1994-95 46
4.1. Impact of educational attainment, literacy and labour market experience on earnings 60
4.2. Impact of continuing education and training and enterprise flexibility on performance
      of workers and enterprises: summary of results from recent surveys and analyses 62
4.3. Selected evaluations of the effectiveness of labour market training
      and employment programmes 64
5.1. A framework for assessing costs and benefits of human capital investment 86

THE IMPORTANCE, SCOPE AND MEASUREMENT OF HUMAN CAPITAL

1. GROWING INTEREST IN HUMAN CAPITAL

Investment in human capital is at the heart of strategies in OECD countries to promote economic prosperity, fuller employment, and social cohesion. Individuals, organisations and nations increasingly recognise that high levels of knowledge, skills and competence are essential to their future security and success. The OECD *Jobs Study* (OECD, 1994) placed particular emphasis on investment in people, in a framework that seeks to extend lifelong learning to all.

There is growing recognition of the importance of investment in human capital through lifelong learning...

Agreement on these principles has heightened political and social expectations for the achievement of far-reaching social and economic goals through greater human capital investment. These general expectations are likely to be unfulfilled unless specific investments in human capital are well designed to meet desired objectives. This requires a good understanding of the nature of human capital, its role in promoting individual, social and economic well-being, and the effectiveness of various measures designed to enhance its supply. At present, these aspects are imperfectly understood, in terms both of analysis of the relationships involved, and of the measurement of human capital formation, stock and returns.

... but such investment will only be productive if it is well understood and therefore well matched with its objectives.

This report therefore aims to clarify what is now known about human capital and how it can be measured. It responds to the 1996 OECD Council Ministerial request:

So, at the request of Ministers the OECD is reporting on what is known about human capital and how it can be measured...

> "to develop an initial set of indicators of human capital investment based on existing data, analyse areas where significant gaps remain in internationally comparable data, identify the cost of development of data collection for new measures and performance indicators, and report to Ministers in 1998 (Communiqué of the OECD Council Meeting at Ministerial Level, May 1996)".

The report addresses these measurement issues in the context of a changing understanding of what constitutes human capital, of its heterogeneous nature and of what kind of human capital formation is best able to achieve public policy objectives. Such understanding is essential in developing useful measures. It has become evident that simplified proxies for human capital formation such as years of initial schooling do not on their own adequately measure the creation of necessary skills and competences, and that only a wider definition can provide clues about where investment is most needed.

... in the framework of indicators of the stock of human capital, its formation through investment, and evidence of returns. In all three areas, the evidence base needs improving.

The remainder of this chapter therefore puts measurement issues in context, by summarising how human capital investment plays a strategic role in OECD societies, by proposing a broad definition of human capital and by considering how that definition can be translated into useful analysis and measurement. Chapters 2-4 use this framework to look at the presently available evidence, respectively, of *stocks*, *investments* and *returns*. A main conclusion from this review is that, despite recent progress, existing indicators and data relating to human capital are still far from being able to adequately capture the scale, changes in, and impacts of human capital, or to be a determinant of policy choices. Analytical and data strategies for rectifying this are proposed in Chapter 5. Finally, in Chapter 6, there is a discussion of some key policy issues raised by the evidence presently available, without suggesting that this evidence on its own offers clear policy prescriptions.

2. THE STRATEGIC ROLE OF HUMAN CAPITAL INVESTMENT

Lifelong learning is now at the top of governments' priorities in promoting growth...

The need for coherent policies to encourage people of all ages to engage in learning is recognised well beyond education ministries, at the highest political levels. The 1997 OECD Council meeting at Ministerial level agreed *"... on the urgent need to implement effective strategies for lifelong learning for all, to strengthen the capacity of individuals to adapt and acquire new skills and competences* (Communiqué of the OECD Council Meeting at Ministerial Level, May 26-27 1997, p. 3)". OECD Labour Ministers, meeting in October 1997, *"... stressed the importance of lifelong learning as a determinant of long-run growth in a knowledge-based economy* (Communiqué of the meeting of the OECD Employment, Labour, and Social Affairs Committee at Ministerial Level, October 14-15 1997, p. 5; and OECD, 1997a)".

... and fostering social cohesion, particularly by tackling unemployment...

Labour Ministers also emphasised the importance of addressing the needs of those whose knowledge and skills are insufficient for full participation in the knowledge-based economy, and whose access to lifelong learning is most limited. A particular priority is investment in the human capital of these groups. The stakes are very high: *"High and persistent unemployment and low pay affecting significant sections of the working-age population risk becoming threats to the social fabric unless they are addressed effectively and in good time* (Communiqué of the Ministerial meeting, *op. cit.*, p. 1)." The problems confronting young people are especially urgent.[1]

... creating a complex set of goals for human capital, which is heterogeneous and requires diverse strategies.

Hence, expectations for human capital investment to deliver key economic and social goals are now high, but also wide-ranging in nature. They concern countries, companies and individuals striving to maintain an edge in intensely competitive situations in which knowledge and skills are critical. At the same time, they concern strategies to overcome unemployment and foster social cohesion. Given the complex set of expectations and objectives associated with human capital investment, it is important to see human capital as a multi-faceted set of characteristics, and investments and their potential results as being equally heterogeneous.

3. DEFINING THE SCOPE OF HUMAN CAPITAL

The concept of human capital has been familiar in economics for at least the past thirty years (*e.g.* Schultz, 1961; Becker, 1964); some trace it back to the work of Adam Smith in the 18th century. This report endorses the value of the concept, rejecting the criticism that such terminology debases human dignity by likening people to packages of knowledge and skill, little different from machinery components. Instead, the concept powerfully emphasises how important people have become, in knowledge- and competence-based economies. It is useful to distinguish between the different forms of "capital" employed in economic activity – in particular physical and human. An important means of optimising the value of each is through understanding the *interaction* of different forms of capital in complex production functions. It follows that measures should ideally be able to describe the quantity, quality, and use of human capital, as well as changes over time; international indicators should do this on a comparative basis.

Human capital can be defined in many ways, but this report adopts the following meaning:

> *"the knowledge, skills, competences and other attributes embodied in individuals that are relevant to economic activity".*

This definition in one sense broadens, and in another sense narrows previous uses of the term. It defines human attributes broadly – not just the level to which a person has been educated, but also the degree to which he or she is able to put a wide range of skills to productive use. At the same time, it narrows the definition to refer only to attributes that have benefits via economic activity. It acknowledges attributes that create better health insofar as this has economic or social spin-offs, for example in containing public healthcare spending, but does not regard the intrinsic personal benefit of being healthy as a return to human capital investment. In other words, it looks at the value of human capital investment for production rather than directly for consumption. This focus on the crucial role that human capital plays in OECD economies, which is a central policy concern, is in no way intended to imply that all forms of learning should be directed to economic ends. It is clear that education, for example, has high "consumption" value, even though that aspect of its benefit is not being examined here.

"Economic" here encompasses all activities that directly or indirectly create wealth or income. Such activities take place primarily within organisations and through individuals in paid work, but also extend to non-market activities that support individuals and employment, such as through voluntary, community, and household work (OECD, 1996a).

Human capital thus constitutes an intangible asset with the capacity to enhance or support productivity, innovation, and employability. It may be augmented, or may decline or become redundant. It is formed through different influences and sources including organised learning activity in the form of education and training. Knowledge, skills, competences, and other attributes combine in different ways according to the individual and the context of use.

Human capital can now be identified as a key factor in economic production...

... and can be defined in terms of various human attributes.

This report focuses on those relevant to economic activity, but takes a broad view of the variety of human abilities that come into play...

... and that are relevant not just to paid work but also to other activities with an economic effect.

There are many ways in which such human attributes are nurtured, combined and deployed...

... and the settings in which human capital are created and used strongly influence its impact, as does the existence of social networks, norms and relationships.

Any strategy to enhance human capital needs to recognise the influence of the social settings in which it is created and used: schools, organisations, labour markets, communities, and national institutions and cultures. However, human capital itself remains an individual characteristic. It should not be confused with *social capital*, which refers to aspects of social life – the existence of networks, norms and relationships – that enable people to act together, create synergies, and build partnerships. Coleman (1990), showed how social capital can influence the ability to acquire human capital, for example when strong communities enhance learning at school. Social capital sets also the context in which human capital can be developed.

Measurement of human capital should pay as much regard to general competences as to intellectual knowledge...

To identify and measure the many different attributes that make up human capital requires a focus directly on what it is that individuals bring to work and economic activity. Attitudes to teamwork, enthusiasm, motivation, and openness to new ideas are at least as important in this regard as "cognitive" abilities directly concerned with knowledge.

... and needs to take a wide view of which attributes can potentially serve economic ends...

Even though human capital as defined here must affect economic or social activity, it can be created through episodes of learning that are not purely job-related in motivation, and which also bring personal benefits. The acquisition of another language, for instance, increasingly represents the creation of human capital. The same education course will be regarded as "vocational" by one person and "non-vocational" by another. Differentiating between the learning that individuals undertake as consumption and as investment is thus difficult in theory and impossible in practice.

... acknowledging that there is an overlap in the skills needed for economic, social and democratic participation.

Moreover, the pursuit of the economic objectives of education can be broadly supportive of its social and democratic aims, and to some extent of cultural and personal goals.[2] The promotion of skills of enquiry and problem-solving, and the motivation and ability to learn and re-learn are relevant to them all, regardless of in which domain they are applied. While human capital implies a focus on the economic sphere, the differences between policies and practices to increase such capital and those directed to other ends can be minor.

4. ANALYSIS AND MEASURES

So measurement of human capital cannot just relate to levels of education...

Measures of "human capital" that have been based on completed years and levels of schooling, and on the return deriving from higher earnings of those with more education, are far from sufficient in relation to a broad definition of human skills and other attributes:

–   A preoccupation with quantitative measures of participation, especially in formal education, neglects learning, knowledge and skills as such – *which* knowledge and skills to promote, under *which* conditions. These are vital policy questions with respect to human capital.

–   The narrow focus on completed educational level and associated qualifications marginalises the issue of depreciation of human capital, since it assumes that qualifications confer permanent gains. Obsolescence is now an important consideration – hence the policy objective of making learning a lifelong activity. Strategies to achieve this are inadequately informed by drawing information only from initial education, where it is most plentiful. Measuring and quantifying the investments by individuals, organisations and governments to maintain or further develop initial human capital endowment is important.

– Frameworks focused on the individual as the main unit of analysis downplay the role of organisations, and their use of human resources. An understanding of the use as well as the potential of human capital must take into account the ability and willingness of firms and other bodies to become "learning organisations".

The analytical chapters below review the best evidence that exists on human capital stocks, investments and returns. The indicators reported have not been developed according to international definitions of human capital *per se* but for a variety of purposes relating in large part to the monitoring of education and training systems. There is thus a large gap between existing evidence and direct measurement of human capital as defined above. That gap is in the process of being closed through major measurement exercises being launched by the OECD. The Organisation is breaking new ground in developing surveys of "cross-curricular competences" among school-age children and of "life skills" among adults. Both of these studies aim to measure knowledge, skills and competences directly, in a broader perspective than existing international tests of student achievement. They will include the domains of motivation and aptitude alongside more specific knowledge, and technical and academic skills.

... yet international indicators are constrained by existing data, which has mainly been designed to monitor education and training systems. The OECD is starting to bridge the gap between such data and genuine indicators of human capital...

It should be acknowledged that this approach looks at human capital formation largely from a "supply side" perspective. In practice, it is relevant to know not just how skills are held by individuals, but how they are sought, used and rewarded in the labour market. As discussed in Chapter 2, it is in principle possible to express an economic measure of the value placed on human capital, but such measures are so far imperfect. Chapter 4 also indirectly measures the use made of human capital, by looking at the realised benefits to individuals. Partly because market signals are often poor, demand for human capital is not readily susceptible to measurement, but this should not cause policy makers to neglect the possibility that skills are being under-utilised rather than under-supplied.

... although information continues to be more closely related to human capital supply than to demand and use in the labour market.

To produce more direct measures of human capital, information about both individuals and settings need to be collected. For *individuals*, clarification is needed empirically of the knowledge, skills, competences and other attributes that enhance productivity, innovation, and employability in different employment-related situations. These imply a large international research agenda. Measures are needed not only of stocks at any one time, but of rates of appreciation and depreciation over time. Such measures should be designed to identify the organisational and economic conditions in which human capital is most likely to be built on or lost.

More research is needed on the one hand to understand how individuals acquire, use and lose human capital...

... and on the other, the respective importance of various settings...

Given the broad definition of human capital, the life-wide *settings* relevant to its creation are also diverse:

- *formal education* (at different levels – early childhood, school-based compulsory education, post-compulsory vocational or general education, tertiary education, adult education etc.);

- *non-formal enterprise-based training* and *public labour market training*;

- the experience acquired *in working life* in different types of organisation and through specific activities such as R&D (the level of skill employed at work can be one of the strongest influences on net human capital formation[3]);

- the large amount of relevant learning that takes place in the more *informal environments* of, for instance, interest networks, families and communities. Learning and preparation for learning that is nurtured within the family and early child care settings provides an important basis for future acquisition of human capital. Learning in the home can potentially be enriched as access to media and information networks expands. Informal environments become increasingly important as countries move towards diverse, individualised forms of learning.

... including the different industrial characteristics of various countries...

The degree to which settings of different types encourage the creation and use of human capital depends to a large extent on specific features of each country such as the way in which education and training are organised and the internal demand for skills. The latter is related to industry structure: for instance, countries that specialise in medium-high tech industries will need a different distribution of human capital than those where industry is polarised between high and low technology. Other relevant factors include the mobility of workers between and within firms, and the degree to which international migration creates a drain or inflow of innovative personnel.

... to examine the returns to human capital investment in different contexts, taking account of its costs...

Measures based on these settings should address, *inter alia*, the dimensions of: *i)* the role of each in producing human capital, quantitatively and qualitatively; *ii)* efficiency measures of each, relating the different settings to cost considerations; *iii)* measures of access and equity; *iv)* investments currently made in these different settings, and by whom; *v)* returns to investments in human capital in these different settings, and for whom. The notion of "returns", as emphasised in Chapter 4, should include both economic and social returns.

... and thus to improve understanding of human capital in its many forms, and its impact at different times and places in people's lives.

The analysis and measurement of human capital is thus not about proposing any simple single measure. It is about building new understandings and typologies, supported by indicators, that address its multi-faceted, dynamic nature. Such understandings need to relate to people's experiences both over time and in various settings: "life-long" as well as "life-wide".

NOTES

1. The OECD Secretary-General has announced a high-level Youth Summit, to be held later in 1998.

2. This is also consistent with the call by the OECD Ministers of Education for "rethinking the way in which much education is currently organised, with the objective of enhancing motivation for lifelong learning and making it accessible to a much wider range of people – including adults returning to learn, the disadvantaged and those with disabilities. Rigid structures and practices – in curricula, grading students by age, fixed and narrow timetables and emphasis on rote learning – often characterise learning in many countries" (Communique of the 1996 meeting of OECD Education Ministers; OECD, 1996b, p. 21).

3. As in the title of Chapter 3 in the most recent OECD *Education Policy Analysis* (1997b) on literacy skills: "Literacy skills: use them or lose them".

REFERENCES

BECKER, G. (1964), "Human capital: A theoretical and empirical analysis, with special reference to education", National Bureau of Economic Research, New York.

COLEMAN, J.S. (1990), *Foundations of Social Theory*, Harvard University Press.

OECD (1994), *The OECD Jobs Study: Evidence and Explanations*, Paris.

OECD (1996a), *Measuring What People Know: Human Capital Accounting for the Knowledge Economy*, Paris.

OECD (1996b), *Lifelong Learning for All*, Paris.

OECD (1997a), "Lifelong learning to maintain employability", Theme 3 of the Draft Analytical Report prepared for the Meeting of Labour Ministers, October 14-15, Paris.

OECD (1997b), *Education Policy Analysis*, Paris.

SCHULTZ, T.W. (1961), "Investment in human capital" , *American Economic Review*, LI:1, pp. 1-22.

MEASURING THE STOCK OF HUMAN CAPITAL

1. THREE APPROACHES TO MEASURING HUMAN CAPITAL STOCK

The level of skills, knowledge and competences held at any one time by individuals can be taken to represent the "stock" of human capital. The total stock within a country can influence its prosperity and international competitiveness. The distribution of knowledge and skills has an important bearing on social participation and access to employment and income. So, governments are interested in both the overall human capital stock and ways in which specific skills and competences are distributed within the population.

The amount of human capital and how it is distributed have important economic and social consequences...

The stock of human capital is heterogeneous: no single type of attribute can adequately represent the many human characteristics that bear on economic activity. It is also important to acknowledge that human capital is in practice more than the sum of its parts, and that the identification and measurement of a finite number of specific skills cannot provide a complete account of human capital stock. The ability of individuals and groups to put these skills together and turn them to productive use, which is related to social capital, is crucial to the overall picture, although hard to measure in any quantitative form.

... but human capital takes many forms, and is more than the sum of its parts.

It is hard enough to measure the stock of individually-held human capital with precision, because the complex set of human attributes that yield economic value cannot be easily quantified. Broadly, three approaches have been used to estimate human capital stocks in the working-age population. The first is to use the highest level of education completed by each adult – or *educational attainment* – as an approximation for human capital. The second is to perform direct tests on adults to determine whether they have certain attributes relevant to economic activity. The third is to look at differences in adults' earnings that appear to be associated with particular individual characteristics, to estimate the market value of these attributes and hence the aggregate value of human capital stock.

Even the sum of individual attributes are difficult to quantify. Different methods can be used:

The educational attainment of the population is at best a proxy measure, since it does not look at human capital attributes directly but rather at the completion of educational levels, which is only broadly associated with some forms of economically-relevant knowledge and competence. It takes account neither of skills

... measuring educational attainment is less satisfactory than testing abilities directly, but it can be hard to test for all relevant attributes...

and competences gained after the completion of formal education nor of the deterioration of abilities through lack of use. Direct tests, on the other hand, can give evidence of various adult characteristics at a given point in time. The complication here is what to measure: human capital is multifaceted, and includes attributes that are difficult to measure at an aggregate level, such as attitudes and motivation.

... an alternative measure of human capital's value is in terms of pay differences, but these do not only reflect different skills...

One way to estimate the extent to which measured attributes constitute human capital in the sense of adding economic value is to look at the reward given to them on the labour market. How much more is a person likely to earn with certain qualifications or competences than without them? By looking at such evidence, it is in principle possible to put a monetary value on human capital stock. However, this indicator rests on the assumption that observed differences in earnings accurately reflect differences in productivity due to educational or measurable skill levels. In practice, such relationships may be weak.

... so in practice the best measures are of attainment, although direct tests are improving.

This chapter looks at available measures of human capital stock across all three measurement approaches. In practice, the best documented evidence is of educational attainment. Direct measures have been weak until recently, but the *International Adult Literacy Survey* (see OECD, Human Resources Development Canada and Statistics Canada, 1997) has for the first time provided a direct comparison of the incidence of certain work-relevant skills in the populations of various countries. Although this evidence covers only some aspects of human capital, it is a useful tool, not least in testing the extent to which the measured skills of adults vary in relation to their educational attainment. The third type of measure, based on market value, is in a much more primitive state of development.

2. MEASURING EDUCATIONAL ATTAINMENT

Qualifications and years of schooling: two measures of attainment

Educational attainment can be expressed as the proportion of adults who have completed each educational level...

Measures of educational attainment are the most commonly-used proxies for human capital. The most straightforward way to describe the educational attainment of the population is in terms of the percentage who have successfully completed various levels of formal education as defined by the *International Standard Classification of Education* (ISCED).[1] This indicator shows, on an internationally standardised basis, how many people have completed each level of initial education. "Level" in this case is defined mainly in relation to the years of study and age associated with an educational cycle, rather than with reference to its content. It does not therefore accurately measure the acquisition of skills or knowledge in a way that can be compared across countries, which have different requirements for completing any given level.

... or a similar measure, the average number of years of schooling completed...

The completion of a given level – say upper secondary – can in practice be associated with somewhat different lengths of study in different countries. So on the assumption that more years of study create more human capital, a "years of schooling" measure is also of interest. An advantage of this measure is that it produces an estimate of a country's human capital stock in a single number – average years of schooling of the adult population. However, this measure is approximate, since it assumes, unrealistically, that a year of education will add a constant quantity of human capital, whether undertaken by a primary school child or a university student.

Figure 2.1 shows educational attainment in OECD countries as measured in these two ways. The overwhelming majority of adults of working age have at least completed primary and lower secondary schooling, so attainment in different countries can most usefully be compared in terms of how many have completed higher levels – upper secondary or above. The proportion who have done so is shown by the total height of each bar. The respective proportions who have only completed upper secondary and who have gone on to complete different kinds of tertiary education are shown by the bars' segments. The "average years of schooling", shown on the right-hand axis, is based on estimates[2] of the number of years spent in completed cycles of primary, secondary and tertiary education by each adult. It does not generally include time in education that did not lead to such a qualification.

... and Figure 2.1 presents both of these measures...

OECD countries differ widely in the average levels of educational attainment of their populations. In most countries, more than 60 per cent of the population aged 25 to 64 has completed at least upper secondary education, and in five countries – the Czech Republic, Germany, Norway, Switzerland and the United States – this proportion exceeds 80 per cent. In other countries, especially in Southern Europe, attainment levels are much lower. In Greece, Ireland, Italy, Luxembourg, Portugal, Spain and Turkey, more than half of the population aged 25-64 years has not completed upper secondary education, and in Portugal the rate is as high as 80 per cent.

... showing that the majority of adults have completed at least upper secondary education in most, but not all countries...

◆ Figure 2.1. **Two measures of educational attainment of the adult population**
Percentage of the population aged 25-64 by the highest completed level of education and estimated average number of years of schooling, 1995

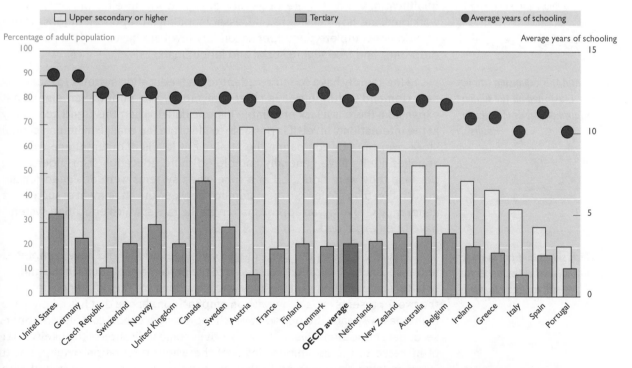

Data for Figure 2.1, p. 98.
Source: Labour Force Survey data (see OECD, 1997b).

Initial education can be measured in terms of years of education, or by level of education successfully completed.

Differences between countries in educational attainment at the tertiary level[3] are even more pronounced. In Canada, 47 per cent of the adult population has a tertiary level of education – with the greater part at the non-university level. In Norway, Sweden and the United States the proportion exceeds 25 per cent, whereas in Austria, Italy and Turkey it is only 8 per cent. However, it should be noted that countries such as Austria, Denmark, Germany, the Netherlands and Switzerland classify many advanced vocational programmes at the upper secondary level. These programmes may be similar in content, orientation and qualifications to programmes that are classified at the tertiary level in, for example, Canada and the United States.

Looking at the educational attainment of populations in terms of average years of schooling (right-hand axis in Figure 2.1) rather than proportions reaching specified levels, does not show great differences in country rankings. Adults in Canada, Germany and the United States have averages of over 13 years; Greek, Irish, Italian and Portuguese adults have the least education, at between 10 and 11 years on average. The Netherlands stands out as a country whose adults have completed on average a relatively lengthy period of schooling, yet a relatively low proportion have upper secondary education. This is due in part to the long duration of some upper secondary and tertiary programmes. In the case of France, the reverse is the case: average duration is low but the proportion with upper secondary attainment is high. This is partly due to the classification of many short programmes at upper secondary level in France.

The changing pattern of attainment

In recent decades, changing labour market and social conditions have led to a clear demand for more education. Upper-secondary and tertiary level qualifications, which were originally designed for an elite minority of the workforce, are now considered necessary for a high proportion of jobs. Those who do not complete the upper secondary level are increasingly regarded as drop-outs, and face severe social and labour market risks.

How rapidly have countries adapted their education systems to meet this new demand? Although it is clear that most have undertaken significant expansion, there is a lack of reliable historic data to chart this trend accurately at the international level. It is possible to illustrate the change in human capital stock over time by comparing the attainment levels of different age cohorts. Younger adults have generally completed more education than older ones, because they were educated at a time when systems were designed for the many rather than the few. So the difference between the attainment of successive generations serves as an approximation for the rate at which education systems have been expanded.

Figure 2.2 shows the percentage of younger adults who have completed upper-secondary education, compared to the percentage of adults in the middle or latter stages of their working lives who have done so. The difference between the two represents expansion, with an emphasis on change that has taken place in the past 15 years, the period in which the younger cohort completed upper-secondary education. This contrast also gives some indication of the likely order of increase in the attainment level of the whole population over the next 20 years (even assuming no further expansion), since a younger cohort with higher attainment will progressively replace less educated older ones.

◆ Figure 2.2. **Percentage of younger (25-34 year olds)
and older adults (45-54) with upper secondary education or higher, 1995**

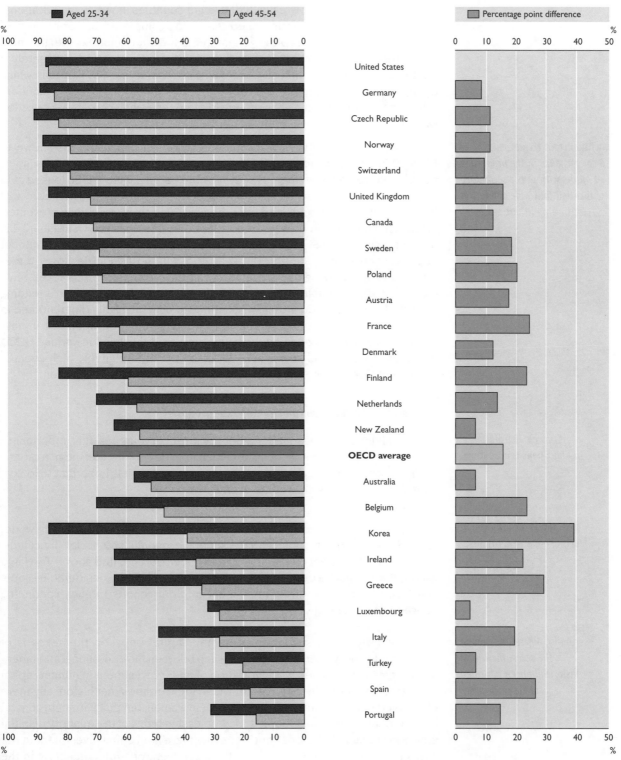

Countries are ranked by percentage of 45-54 year olds
with upper secondary attainment or higher.
Data for Figure 2.2, p. 99.
Source: Labour Force Survey data (see OECD, 1997*b*).

*Younger adults are more qualified,
but the generation gap varies greatly across countries.*

... although the present rate of this expansion varies greatly among countries...

The difference in attainment between generation is not always great. In the United States, it is zero, largely because an early expansion in high-school participation created high levels of attainment in generations that are now in the middle or later stages of working life. In eight countries, however, an additional 20 per cent of the population aged 25-34 has completed upper secondary education compared to the older generation. In the three countries with the most rapid expansion, Greece, Korea, and Spain, this represents approximately a doubling of the attainment rate. Conversely, in a country such as France in which a majority in older generations were already completing upper-secondary education, rapid expansion has produced more than a halving of the proportion who do not reach this level (from 38 per cent to 14 per cent).

... with current trends pointing to a convergence in the proportion of adults with upper-secondary education, but wide differences continuing at tertiary level.

Most of the countries with the fastest rate of expansion (as shown in Figure 2.2) are also those whose present attainment rates across the adult population are below average, as shown by the bars in Figure 2.1. So looked at in terms of upper-secondary completion, considerable convergence in the stock of human capital can be projected over the next 20 years. Calculations presented elsewhere show that in present trends, for those countries shown in Figure 2.2, only Portugal and Turkey are likely to have a minority of working-age adults without upper-secondary education in the year 2015.[4] In most countries, over three-quarters of the working-age population will have completed this level. Such convergence is inevitable at an educational level for which participation is tending towards the universal. Countries will continue to be more highly differentiated in terms of tertiary-level attainment: as shown in Figure 2.1, between one in nine and one in two working-age adults have completed this level in various OECD countries. There is still scope here for countries with relatively high average attainment levels to preserve this differential through further expansion.

The pattern of attainment among different groups

Uneven distribution of qualifications is of concern:

As lifelong learning for all is a priority in OECD countries, it is important to ensure that no subgroups are being excluded from developing their human capital. So, in measuring the stock of educational qualifications, it is important to look at their distribution as well as at the overall level.

... first, the lower attainment levels of older generations...

One concern is over generational differences: in a rapidly changing world, less-educated older groups can face serious economic and social difficulties. Variations in attainment by age have already been documented above. To a large extent, these differences represent historic trends. There is considerable scope, however, to correct for under-attainment in older cohorts through continuing education and training.

... secondly, differences among the sexes: men have historically been educated to higher levels...

Secondly, the distribution of human capital between the sexes is of considerable policy interest. A significant gap between the educational attainment levels of men and women is an indication of under-investment in human capital for a sizeable part of the population. The evidence shows that historically there has indeed been such an under-investment in women, but that it is not in general being repeated for young people today, at least in terms of the quantity of initial education (although this does not mean that there is an equal investment in the sexes in other respects). Looking at the attainment of adults presently in the workforce (representing historic graduation trends), an average (see Table A2.6 in the Annex) of 63 per cent of men and 57 per cent of women have upper secondary education across OECD countries. This relatively small gap of 6 percentage points rises to above 10 percentage points in eight countries, including the four OECD countries – Austria, Czech Republic, Germany and Switzerland – with the strongest "dual" systems of apprenticeship-based upper secondary education.

But for those graduating from upper secondary education now, women represent a higher proportion (85 per cent on average in 1995) of the population at the relevant completion age than men (80 per cent) [see indicator G1.1 in OECD, 1997*b*, p. 324]. Countries with dual systems no longer appear to have a general bias towards male completion, although Switzerland is one of the remaining countries with more men (84 per cent) completing than women (75 per cent).

... although today's young women are about as likely to complete a given level...

A third relevant aspect of the distribution of attainment is the degree to which educational disadvantage perpetuates itself through generations. In societies that aim for equality of opportunity, the correlation between the educational fortunes of individuals and of their parents can be disturbingly high. Limits to intergenerational mobility in this sense can create problems both in terms of equity and in terms of raising the overall level of human capital stock.

... and thirdly, the passing down of educational underachievement from parent to offspring...

One useful indicator of such mobility examines the probability of obtaining a tertiary level of education, for groups whose parents have reached each respective level of attainment. The difference between the chance of getting a tertiary education if at least one parent got one, and the chance of doing so if neither parent completed secondary school, can be expressed as a ratio. This ratio expresses the "Intergenerational Education Gap". In ten countries surveyed,[5] the ratio ranges from 2.0 in Australia, to 5.8 in Poland. That is to say, having a well-educated parent makes one between twice as likely and six times as likely to obtain tertiary education than if one has poorly-educated parents. Comparing older and younger generations of adults, and the relationship in each case of their level of education to that of their parents, it appears that these inequalities tend to be increasing in countries where they are less severe, while narrowing in the other countries where they are higher (Table A2.7 in the Annex).

... which varies in degree among countries, although there is some evidence of convergence.

Four limitations with educational attainment as a proxy for human capital

While educational attainment can be a useful tool for comparing one feature of the human capital stock, it is important to bear in mind its limitations. These can be summarised as follows:

Educational attainment as a measure of human capital is limited:

- Even though attainment of an educational level usually requires some demonstration of knowledge and skills in order to pass courses and/or grades, these requirements vary widely among countries, and have not been designed to measure human capital as defined in this report. So even though there may be some correlation between attainment and relevant skills, knowledge and competence, school completion does not guarantee these attributes.

... first, because completion of schooling does not certify a consistent set of skills...

- Attainment only certifies education undertaken as part of a completed cycle of formal education. It ignores, for example, learning on courses that do not lead to a recognised qualification or less formal adult education, as well as enterprise-based training.

... second, because it ignores less formal learning...

... third, because skills can depreciate...

– Even insofar as completing a level of education certifies certain knowledge and skills at time of completion, it does not follow that these attributes can be measured in adults by looking at their educational background, often from several decades earlier. Their experiences in adulthood can both add to educational attainment through formal and informal learning, and subtract from it if skills are lost through disuse.

... and fourth, because it can be hard to compare attainment by economic category.

– In cases where data on attainment cannot be broken down by industry sector, occupation or other economically-relevant categories, an alternative is to use data on the percentage of persons holding positions at various skill levels in particular occupations classified according to the International Standard Classification of Occupations (ISCO-88). Such comparisons can raise comparability problems because of variations in the application of this standard to national occupation codes.

3. MEASURING ADULT SKILLS DIRECTLY

A *new type of direct measure*

A new direct measure of an aspect of human capital is the International Adult Literacy Survey (IALS), in which adults were tested on three literacy scales, and assigned to one of five levels of literacy on each scale...

An alternative to measuring the human capital stock via educational qualifications or years of schooling is to assess the skills of adults directly. The results of the *International Adult Literacy Survey* (see OECD, Human Resources Development Canada and Statistics Canada, 1997) provide a novel approach to the measurement of skills and competences in an international context. The survey has so far been carried out in 12 OECD Member countries, and creates a model that could be used to test a range of attributes related to human capital. Its main features are:

– Detailed interviews with a large sample of the working-age population (between 2, 000 and 8, 000 per country) in their homes, consisting of both a test of respondents' ability to carry out certain tasks and a gathering of background information on the characteristics of participants such as age, socio-economic status and participation in various educational and other activities that may be associated with human capital formation.

– The definition of a number of domains of the type of skill being tested, in this case "prose literacy", "document literacy" and "quantitative literacy" (see box). In each domain, respondents are required to use the skills in question to perform tasks that simulate situations that they are likely to confront in everyday life, including in a work context.

– The construction of a continuous scale of scores (from 0 to 500) representing tasks of varying difficulties in each domain. Based on the tasks performed, each respondent is assigned a single score for each domain, which represents the highest level of task that they are likely to succeed in, with a probability of 80 per cent.

– A grouping of these results into levels of performance from 1 to 5, with level 1 representing those who fail to perform at a specified minimum level (see box). These levels emphasise that there is no single threshold at which adults can be said to have a skill relevant to human capital, but rather that may have it to a greater or lesser degree. This is particularly relevant in the case of literacy, since many past analyses have assumed that everybody was either fully literate or fully illiterate. The levels of literacy in the International Adult Literacy Survey (IALS) represent the varying degrees of complexity in the components of literacy skill needed in different situations in which written materials are used.

The International Adult Literacy Survey *identified literacy skills to cover demands at work, in the home and the community. Each literacy domain is divided into five task levels of varying difficulty*:

Literacy domains

Prose literacy: the knowledge and skills that are required to understand and use information from newspapers, fiction and expository text.

Document literacy: the knowledge and skills that are required to locate and use the information contained in official forms, timetables, maps and charts.

Quantitative literacy: the knowledge and skills that are required to apply mathematical operations in printed materials.

Literacy levels

Level 1: able at most to locate a single straightforward piece of information in simple written materials.

Level 2: able to locate pieces of information based on simple matching requiring a low level of inference.

Level 3: able to use written materials making low-level inferences taking account of multiple pieces of information.

Level 4: able to perform multiple-feature or less straightforward tasks using complex information.

Level 5: able to perform complex tasks combining several pieces of information that must be searched for in the written material.

A similar approach is now being developed by the OECD in partnership with a number of Member countries with respect to "life skills", in domains such as problem-solving, teamwork and information technology. This methodology is applicable to the measurement of a wide range of attributes associated with human capital. As such tests are not inexpensive, however, governments need to define carefully which kinds of skill they would most like to measure.

This approach could now be extended to other kinds of "life skills".

High literacy shortfalls, especially among older cohorts

Although there is no single cut-off point that defines whether a person is literate, the results of the International Adult Literacy Survey (IALS) show a worrying degree of under-performance. Performance at literacy level 3 is generally considered to be desirable in order to avoid difficulties in coping with social and economic life in a modern democratic society. Although those on levels 1 and 2 may be able to read and understand simple materials, they have difficulties with the more complex tasks that are now required of workers and citizens. So the proportion of the population performing at levels 1 and 2 can be taken to represent a shortfall relative to the desirable minimum.

IALS does not set a single literacy threshold, but identifies adults whose skills are likely to be inadequate for the modern world...

... with typically between one-third and one-half of OECD adult populations judged likely to face literacy problems...

Figure 2.3 shows that of those tested, between one-quarter and just over one-half of OECD working-age populations perform below this desirable minimum – at levels 1 and 2 – except in Poland, where the proportion is above three-quarters. These figures apply to the document scale, but results on the other two scales are broadly similar. Such a shortfall indicates a need to improve skills among a wide section of the population, not just a small minority of low-literate adults. The pattern of distribution varies considerably between countries. For example, results for the United States and the United Kingdom are more polarised than elsewhere, in that higher than average proportions of the population of these countries show low literacy levels (levels 1 and 2), but relatively high proportions also perform at the top two levels (levels 4 and 5).[6]

... a disproportionate number of whom are older adults...

As with low educational attainment, a disproportionate amount of the literacy shortfall occurs among older adults who missed out on the recent expansion of education systems. Figure 2.3 shows that in most cases a considerably higher proportion of 46-55 year olds than 16-25 year olds have low literacy skills. This is particularly true in two countries, Belgium (Flanders) and Ireland, where the generation gap in educational attainment (see Figure 2.2 above) is also high. Conversely in the United States, where older cohorts are just as likely to have completed secondary school as younger ones, their literacy skills are not inferior. However, as shown below, differences in educational attainment cannot explain all the difference in adult literacy performance.

... with low skills not just being associated with lack of education, but also with a lack of use of particular skills.

The evidence from IALS and previous North American literacy studies suggests that both depreciation and appreciation of skills takes place over the life-cycle. Depreciation of skills is often associated with long-term unemployment and economic inactivity, so there is a risk of greater social polarisation. There is also evidence of a significant mismatch between the skills workers possess and those required in the jobs that are available. Against a background of an ageing workforce and population, the issue of upgrading and renewing skills has grown in importance. The IALS results suggest that literacy scores may be dependent on the literacy demands of cultural and workplace environments, reflecting the degree to which adults build on or lose skills initially acquired at school.

Literacy by economic sector

Low literacy is particularly common among agricultural workers, but in some countries it is higher for manufacturing workers.

One advantage of direct measures of human capital is that they allow comparisons of its distribution among workers in different parts of the economy. As illustrated in Figure 2.4, a disproportionate number of low-literate workers work in agriculture. In most countries a relatively higher percentage of agricultural and mining workers perform at levels 1 and 2 (in Poland, the percentage is at 90 per cent). However, variations across sectors differ considerably from one country to another. For example, in Germany and Switzerland (French and German speaking), manufacturing workers are considerably less likely to have low literacy than agricultural workers, whereas in the United States the converse is true. Financial and business services show a high proportion performing at the upper literacy levels, about 30 per cent on average, and this rises to about half of such workers in Canada and Sweden.

◆ Figure 2.3. *Adults performing above and below an adequate threshold of literacy, 1994-95*

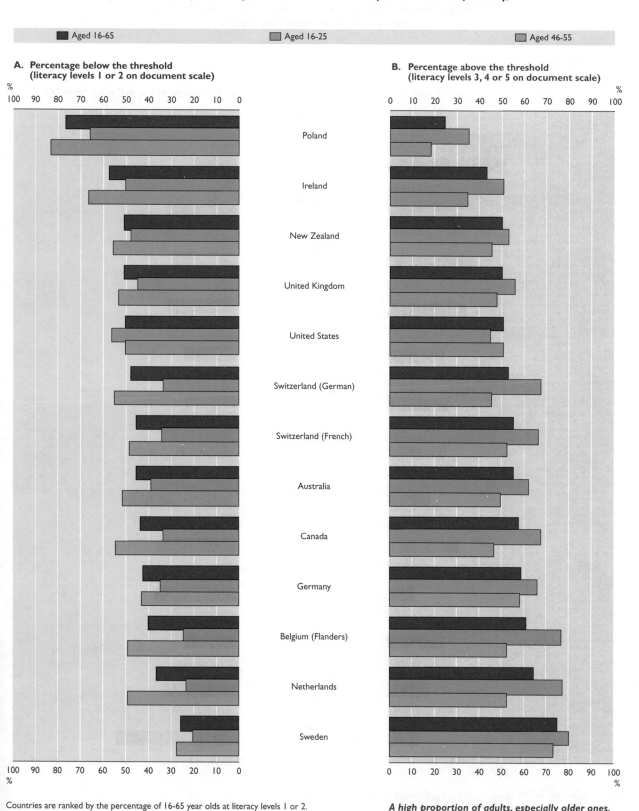

| ■ Aged 16-65 | ■ Aged 16-25 | ■ Aged 46-55 |

A. Percentage below the threshold
(literacy levels 1 or 2 on document scale)

B. Percentage above the threshold
(literacy levels 3, 4 or 5 on document scale)

Countries are ranked by the percentage of 16-65 year olds at literacy levels 1 or 2.
Data for Figure 2.3, p. 99.
Source: International Adult Literacy Survey.

A high proportion of adults, especially older ones, lack the literacy skills needed in knowledge-oriented societies.

25

◆ Figure 2.4. **Literacy levels of workers in different economic sectors**
*Percentage of workers aged 16-65 with low (levels 1 or 2) and high (levels 4 or 5)
literacy levels on document scale, 1994-95*

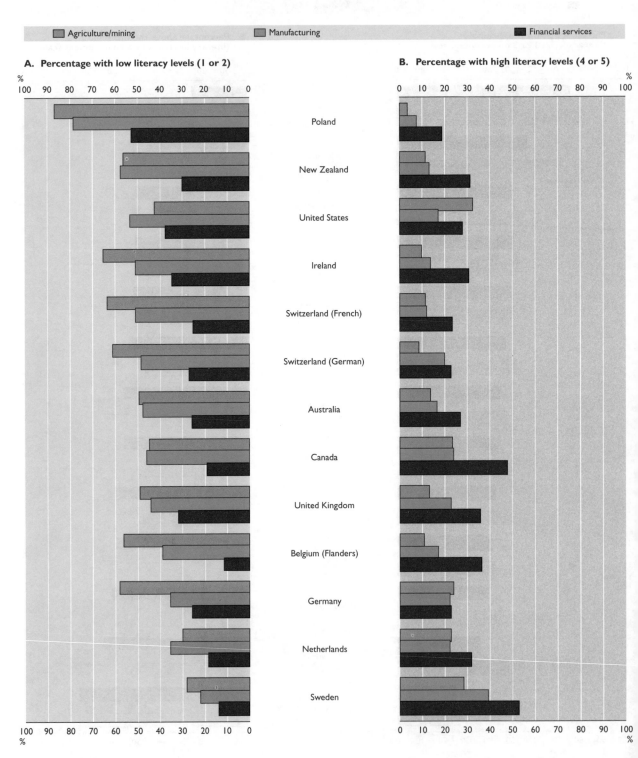

Countries are ranked by the percentage of workers in manufacturing
at literacy levels 1 or 2.
Data for Figure 2.4, p. 100.
Source: International Adult Literacy Survey.

*The literacy shortfall is particularly high in some
sectors such as agriculture, but it varies greatly in
manufacturing.*

Literacy, educational attainment and student achievement

As the first direct measure of its type, the *International Adult Literacy Survey* not only offers valuable direct evidence of the incidence of human capital, but also gives an initial approximation of the degree of correspondence between education and skills in adulthood. Its results show that the overall correlation between educational attainment and literacy performance within each country is high. This finding, however, must be qualified in two ways. First, a substantial proportion of the population perform at literacy levels that do not correspond to their educational level. Second, the average literacy performance of people with similar attainment in different countries varies greatly.

Although people who do not complete secondary education most commonly have low literacy skills, a substantial minority in most countries and almost 75 per cent of Swedes reach level 3 or higher in the document literacy scale (see page 147 in OECD and Statistics Canada, 1995). Conversely, while people with tertiary education generally show high literacy skills, some 20 per cent of graduates from the United States and German-speaking Switzerland are at levels 1 and 2. Clearly a good education is neither wholly necessary nor sufficient for the development of literacy skills useful for life.

Better-educated adults tend to be more literate, but this must be qualified in two ways:

... first, in some countries many less-educated people have high literacy, and in others many better-educated ones have low literacy...

◆ Figure 2.5. **Adult literacy and educational attainment**
Mean document scores for persons aged 16-65 on a scale with a range of 500 points, by level of educational attainment, 1994-95

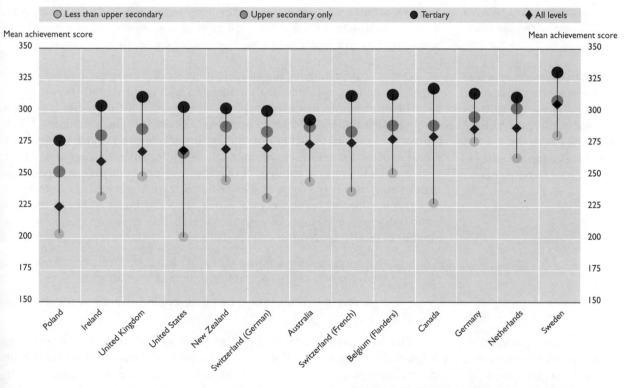

In each country, better-educated persons are on average more literate, but average literacy of individuals with the same educational level varies widely across countries.

Countries are ranked by the value of mean achievement score for all levels.
Data for Figure 2.5, p. 101.
Source: International Adult Literacy Survey,

... and secondly, across countries, the same level of education yields on average very different literacy outcomes...

However, the degree to which educational attainment translates into literacy is highly variable from one country to another. Figure 2.5 shows the average literacy scores for people with different levels of education. Although within each country more education gives on average a higher score, looking across countries the picture is less consistent. For example, a German without upper-secondary education scores on average higher than an American high school graduate, and Swedish upper-secondary graduates score better than adults with tertiary qualifications below university level in all six English-speaking countries in the survey. So in terms of creating literacy skills for life, different education systems perform at very different levels.

... while there appears to be no close correspondence between countries' scores on international tests of student achievement and subsequent literacy in adulthood.

Another way of measuring the output of these systems is in terms of student achievement – direct measures of the knowledge and skills on an internationally comparable basis. The International Association for the Evaluation of Educational Achievement provides such measures, most recently through the *Third International Mathematics and Science Survey* (TIMSS). Such achievement measures, however, measure only certain aspects of useful skills learned at school, and neglect aspects such as self-discipline, problem-solving and other general characteristics relevant to human capital. It is notable that in countries such as Sweden and Germany, adults score well above average in quantitative literacy whereas school students show only medium performance in mathematics scores at age 13.

4.   ESTIMATING THE MARKET VALUE OF HUMAN CAPITAL

Labour markets place a particular value on human capital through wages.

Individual characteristics such as educational attainment and measured skills are seen as being relevant to the functioning of individuals in the labour market. In order to calculate fully the stock of human capital, however, some measure is needed of how much, in practice, such attributes are worth in economic terms.

Earnings differences can be used to estimate the total economic value of human capital, if it is assumed that they are related to productivity differences, and that less skilled workers are valued as roughly equal...

One way of quantifying the human capital stock is therefore by aggregating the higher earnings of individuals associated with particular attributes. There have been attempts to devise a *labour-income-based* (LIB) measure, based on earnings differentials associated with levels of educational attainment.[7] The ratio of the earnings of higher-educated to lower-educated workers provides a measure of the former's human capital. By weighting different segments of the workforce by the ratio of earnings at different levels of education, it is possible to derive an index of the value of average human capital stock.[8] Labour-income-based measures of human capital stock have the merit of being directly comparable with measures of physical capital. This approach depends on a number of crucial assumptions which include:

–   that earnings from employment provide a good indication of marginal labour productivity and returns to human capital; and

–   a perfect substitution between different individuals with a low level of human capital.

... and although these assumptions may not always hold, "labour-income based" measures of human capital can be useful...

The first assumption may be less true of countries where earnings differentials are strongly influenced by institutional factors such as bargaining and minimum-wage provisions. The second assumption may be questionable on the grounds that human capital is very different from one individual to another and that obstacles exist to the mobility or substitutability of labour at a low level of educational attainment. However, labour-income-based (LIB) measures have the advantage of allowing for changes in the relative productivity of workers over time and across countries (on the assumption that earnings are a good guide to marginal productivity), and they do not assume that workers at the same level of educational attainment necessarily have the same level of skill. If, at a given level of attainment, individuals have studied different subjects, their productivity and their earnings can vary to reflect this.

Measures of this kind have so far been restricted to individual countries, but the studies to date are instructive. Mulligan and Sala-i-Martin (1995) have used a measure based on educational attainment of the labour force and the share of different groups in labour income. They found that across states in the US, those with the lowest level of human capital stock in the initial period had the highest growth over time. They also found that for the period 1940-90, the stock of human capital grew twice as quickly in the United States than would have been indicated by measures based on average years of schooling alone. Furthermore, the dispersion of the stock of human capital increased across the United States during the 1980s, whereas the dispersion in average years of schooling narrowed. This last finding is used to challenge the conclusion that earnings inequality in the United States during the 1980s could not have been related to human capital because its distribution was becoming more equal.

... showing, for example, that pay inequalities due to human capital differences may be growing even though there is less inequality in the quantity of schooling...

Labour-income-based measures of human capital stock only take account of the market value of human capital. One study by Jorgenson and Fraumeni (1993) has estimated both the market and non-market values of human capital for the United States in terms of a future stream of additional earnings for different groups according to age, gender and labour market status. An imputed value for non-market time is added to this. Ahlroth, Björklund and Forslund (1997) use a similar estimation for Sweden. Investment in the stock of human capital, when account is taken of its impact outside the market, may represent a greater value than physical capital and a considerably greater amount than the value of time spent at work. Ahlroth, Björklund and Forslund found that, even if leisure income and income taxes are excluded, the value of human capital stock exceeds that of physical capital.[9] This also raises some fundamental issues related to the treatment of education expenditure as an investment or consumption in the context of national accounts which are discussed in Chapters 5 and 6 below.

... while calculations that add in non-market value appear to show that the stock of human capital could be worth more than physical capital.

5. BEYOND INDIVIDUAL CHARACTERISTICS

A nation's human capital stock cannot be fully measured by the sum of the attributes of individuals. In practice, the ways in which skills and knowledge are developed and applied in an economy depend also on a host of other variables including social capital and the culture of organisations. It is difficult to aggregate these variables into reliable measures.

The social and organisational context in which human capital is deployed cannot be easily measured...

However, one tangible activity that helps influence the degree to which human competence can be translated into productive economic activity is investment in the development of knowledge. So, in addition to measures of human capital stock based on educational attainment of the population as a whole, it is useful to compare the stock of highly-skilled "knowledge producers" in the economy. One way of measuring this is to compare the number of research and development staff relative to the labour force. Table 2.1 shows that there are wide variations in the investment in R&D expressed in these terms, by a factor of more than two among countries at similar stages of economic development.

... but one valuable indicator of social investment in "knowledge producers" is the number of R&D workers, which varies greatly.

Table 2.1. **Number of research and development employees**[1] **per 10 000 individuals in the labour force, 1994**

	R&D employees
Japan[2]	81
United States (1993)	74
Norway (1993)	69
Sweden (1993)	68
Australia	64
Finland (1993)	61
France	59
Germany (1993)	58
Iceland	58
Belgium	53
Canada (1993)	53
Ireland	52
United Kingdom	50
Netherlands	48
Denmark (1993)	47
Switzerland (1992)	46
New Zealand (1993)	37
Austria (1993)	34
Italy	33
Spain	30
Hungary	28
Poland	27
Czech Republic	26
Greece (1993)	20
Portugal (1992)	20
Turkey	7
Mexico (1993)	5
Country average (unweighted)	45

1. Including university graduate support staff for some countries.
2. Figure for Japan is overestimated in the case of the business sector.
Source: OECD Directorate for Science, Technology and Industry (DSTI) database, November 1997.

6. CONCLUSIONS

Human capital is unevenly distributed across and within countries...

This chapter has shown marked variation across OECD countries in levels of human capital stock, whether measured by educational attainment or by direct tests of adult literacy. The results for alternative measures are not always the same; North American countries have the highest attainment, and certain north European countries score best on measured literacy – reinforcing the point that human capital is heterogeneous and cannot be expressed through any single indicator. Moreover, human capital is unevenly distributed within countries. Evidence from the *International Adult Literacy Survey* (IALS) shows high levels of low skill among the adult population in many OECD countries – particularly among older workers.

... and although indicators have hitherto been focused on educational attainment, direct measures promise to deepen the understanding needed to address shortfalls in human capital stock.

A range of human capital stock measures have been illustrated here. Educational attainment will continue to be used widely because it continues to be the most extensively available indicator of human capital stock in a wide range of different data sources, and because it is positively correlated with directly measured skills and with wages. However, direct skill measures provide a more accurate measure of human capital at different points in the life-cycle – one which better reflects learning, training and skill attrition throughout life. The *International Adult Literacy Survey* represents only the beginning of an international effort to measure skills directly. The development of a wider range of skill measures, through the *International Life Skills Survey* is discussed further in Chapter 5.

STOCK INDICATORS

Indicator	What it shows	Usefulness and limitations	Data availability and sources	References in this volume
a) Educational attainment of the population aged 25-64	Percentage who have gained upper-secondary and tertiary level qualifications	Internationally standardised measure of educational level reached. But does not measure any specific set of knowledge and skills	OECD collects comprehensive data on all countries, based on *International Standard Classification of Education* (ISCED) definitions	Figure 2.1 and Table A2.1 in the Annex
b) Average "years of schooling" of the population aged 25-64	Estimated average number of years spent in completed episodes of primary, secondary and tertiary education	Gives single figure for stock of human capital based on attainment. But takes a year of education as a constant unit regardless of level. And same limits as a) above	Source data as for a), but relies on estimating the average number of years associated with each attainment level	Figure 2.1 and Table A2.1 in the Annex
c) Educational attainment of the adult population broken down by age	Percentage who have gained at least upper-secondary education in the 25-34 and 35-64 age-bands	Indicates generational differences due to changes over time in youth attainment rates. But does not separate out the effect of adult education	Source data as for a)	Figure 2.2 and Table A2.2 in the Annex
d) Educational attainment and qualification rates broken down by gender	Differences between men and women i) in upper-secondary attainment among adults aged 25-64 and ii) in current upper-secondary qualification rate	Compares historic gender biases with present trends in education systems	Attainment rates: as for a) Qualification rates: *Education at a Glance – OECD Indicators* (1997), p. 324	Table A2.6 in Annex
e) "Intergenerational Education Gap"	Ratio of i) chance of gaining tertiary qualification if one's parents reached this level to ii) chance of gaining tertiary qualification if parents did not complete secondary school	Gives an indication of educational mobility between generations, which has a bearing both on equality of opportunity and the prospect of improving overall human capital stock	Analysis of *International Adult Literacy Survey* gives results for eleven countries. Reported in de Broucker and Underwood (1997)	Table A2.7 in the Annex
f) Overall distribution of literacy skills in adult population	Percentage performing at each of five levels of measured literacy in three domains	Gives a direct measure of a set of skills with economic relevance. But only indicative of how education and other experiences account for these skills	*International Adult Literacy Survey* results for 12 countries, published by the OECD in 1995 and 1997	Figure 2.3 and Table A2.3 in the Annex
g) Literacy shortfalls by age	Percentage of 16-25 year-olds and 46-55 year olds on bottom two literacy levels	Shows how in some countries low literacy is concentrated in older cohorts, partly because of their lower educational attainment. But low literacy can also arise from skill deterioration	Ditto	Figure 2.3 and Table A2.3 in the Annex

STOCK INDICATORS (continued)

Indicator	What it shows	Usefulness and limitations	Data availability and sources	References in this volume
h) Literacy by sector of economic activity	Percentage of workers in selected industries with high (levels 4/5) and low (levels 1/2) literacy levels on document scale	Shows how literacy tends to be highest in more knowledge-based industries	*International Adult Literacy Survey* results for 12 countries, published by the OECD in 1995 and 1997	Figure 2.4 and Table A2.4 in the Annex
i) Literacy by educational attainment	Average literacy score in each country of people with respective attainment levels	Shows how much difference education makes to literacy in each country, and also allows comparisons across countries of literacy among people with similar educational attainment	Ditto	Figure 2.5 and Table A2.5 in the Annex

NOTES

1. It should be noted that the existing ISCED classification system has been found to be weak in many important respects of international comparability and is currently being revised. Hence, measures of human capital based on completed ISCED levels need to be treated with caution, especially where similar types or levels of programmes are being classified according to different currently defined ISCED levels.

2. Such estimates are not perfect; they are arrived at by looking at the highest educational level that an adult has completed, and then assuming the number of years of education it has taken to reach that level. One way in which some countries (*e.g.* Ireland and the Nordic countries) systematically underestimate the average number of years of schooling is by assuming that all children start formal education only at the compulsory school age, whereas in fact some start earlier.

3. Tertiary-level education describes formal education provided after completion of upper secondary level – typically from the age of 17-19 years. Tertiary level includes both non-university and university programmes.

4. Detailed projections are presented in *Education Policy Analysis* (OECD, 1997*a*), pp. 36-39. This analysis shows that upper-secondary attainment in Spain would not quite reach 50 per cent if youth attainment remained at the present level for 25-29 year olds, but continuing expansion is likely. Even in Portugal, where only 20 per cent of the population had upper-secondary education in 1995, a rapid expansion in the proportion of young people graduating at this level could potentially raise adult attainment above 50 per cent within 20 years.

5. Through the background questions asked in the *International Adult Literacy Survey* (see OECD, Human Resources Development Canada and Statistics Canada, 1997) analysed by de Broucker and Underwood (1997).

6. Subtle differences in survey design and implementation, and in the pattern of non-response across languages and cultures, do introduce some error into the literacy estimates. Where appropriate, standard errors are therefore reported in the tables based on IALS. Re-weighting of data and analysis of non-respondent groups in the selected national samples revealed that the achieved samples were broadly representative of the total population and the results were not unduly biased by the level of non-response.

7. The value of human capital stock is estimated by taking the weighted sum of all workers or groups where the weights correspond to average earnings of each worker/group divided by the numeraire which is average earnings of zero-skill workers. Human capital values may be estimated for economically inactive members of the population by assigning "shadow wages" to such individuals based on their educational attainment or labour force experience.

8. Marchand and Thélot (1997) have estimated an index of human capital for France over the last 200 years using numbers of economically active persons and an estimate of quality of labour. The latter is based on estimates of productivity by years of formal schooling completed in the adult population aged 15-64. They estimate that the stock of human capital has tripled over this time, and that about half of this increase can be accounted for by increased quality of labour, and the other half by increased numbers of economically active persons.

9. A recent report of work in progress by the World Bank (1995) used a methodology for estimating the stock of human, natural and produced assets in various countries. In relation to human capital, a monetary value was ascribed to an estimate of the stock based on an estimated share of labour in the future income pool that today's population might expect, other things being equal, discounted at 4 per cent per annum. Future lifetime income was estimated for each age-group and a deduction was made in respect of the share of natural and produced assets in this income pool. The residual was estimated as going to human capital. On the basis of these estimates, human capital was estimated to represent on average 67 per cent of total wealth in high-income countries with about one sixth accounted for by produced and natural assets each.

REFERENCES

AHLROTH, S., BJÖRKLUND, A. and FORSLUND, A. (1997), "The output of the Swedish education sector", *Review of Income and Wealth*, Series 43, No. 1, March.

de BROUCKER, P. and UNDERWOOD, K. (1997), "An indicator of equity: The probability of attaining a post-secondary credential by the level of parents' education", Working Paper for Network B of the OECD INES project, Centre for Education Statistics, Statistics Canada, Ottawa.

JORGENSON, D. and FRAUMENI, B. (1993), "Education and productivity growth in a market economy", *Atlantic Economic Journal*, June, Vol. 21, No. 2.

MARCHAND, O. and THELOT, C. (1997), "Formation de la main-d'œuvre et capital humain en France depuis deux siècles", Les dossiers Éducation et Formations, No. 80, ministère de l'Éducation nationale, de l'Enseignement supérieur et de la Recherche, DEP, March.

MULLIGAN, C.B. and SALA-I-MARTIN, X. (1995), "Measuring aggregate human capital", NBER Working Paper No. 5016, Cambridge, Mass.

OECD (1997*a*), *Education Policy Analysis*, Paris.

OECD (1997*b*), *Education at a Glance – OECD Indicators*, Paris.

OECD and Statistics Canada (1995) *Literacy, Economy and Society, Results of the First International Adult Literacy Survey*, Paris and Ottawa.

OECD, Human Resources Development Canada and Statistics Canada (1997), *Literacy Skills for the Knowledge Society – Further Results from the International Adult Literacy Survey*, Paris.

WORLD BANK (1995), *Monitoring Environmental Progress: A Report on Work in Progress*, Washington, DC, Chapter 8.

INVESTMENT IN HUMAN CAPITAL

1. MEASURING THE RESOURCES INVESTED

In the long run, the stock of human capital depends on the rate at which individuals acquire knowledge, skills, competences and other attributes, as well as on the extent to which they manage to retain them once acquired. As with physical capital, therefore, both investment and depreciation rates are of interest. While the latter can be difficult to measure, the processes by which individuals build up various kinds of human capital in childhood and adulthood need to be understood by those seeking to strengthen the human capital base.

Human capital formation can be measured in terms of child and adult learning, although depreciation is also relevant...

Investment in human capital takes place over the course of people's lives in a wide range of settings – including in the family, at school and at work. The quantity of human capital investment can most readily be measured through two resources devoted to learning: money and time. This chapter aims to complement Chapter 2 by providing evidence of the money and time being devoted to increasing the human capital stock.

The amount of money spent by individuals, companies and governments on training and education, and the time spent by participants in courses of study, serve as useful approximations of human capital formation. In practice, the concepts of time and money investments overlap, since forgone earnings can be an important element of the cost of learning that takes place beyond compulsory schooling. Both time and money expended are indirect measures of capital formation, since a dollar of spending or an hour of study produce highly variable types and quantities of human capital. They also take insufficient account of learning outside formal programmes, for which resource investments are less visible. Such measures can, however, provide some idea of how different countries structure human capital investment, in terms of type, level and duration. A country may have a relatively low level of human capital stock as measured by years of schooling or educational attainment, for example, but nevertheless make large investments in each student, or have a relatively high level of participation in learning beyond schooling, including job-related training.

... such investment can be measured in terms of both money and time devoted to study, although this neglects less formal learning.

2. FINANCIAL MEASURES OF INVESTMENT

Measures of spending on human capital investment are uneven, with data on formal education the easiest to aggregate.

It is not easy to measure adequately all of the many forms of investment in human capital. Public and private spending on formal education is relatively well documented. Spending by enterprises on job-related training programmes is also possible to quantify, although some less formal work-based learning can be hard to distinguish. The ways in which families devote resources to children are important in determining lifetime learning patterns, but it is impossible to calculate how much overall spending on children should be attributed to human capital investment. This section looks at those aspects of human capital formation that can be quantified, without claiming to present a complete picture.

Expenditure on education and training: two measures

Spending on formal education and training can be measured either in total relative to GDP or per-student relative to GDP per capita.

A substantial proportion of the resources of OECD economies – between 4.5 and 9 per cent of GDP – is devoted to running formal systems of education and training. Most of this expenditure is from public sources, but in many countries a substantial portion is private. Total spending on education as a percentage of GDP gives an idea of the overall effort in terms of tax and private outlays devoted to such investment, but hides the factors that lie behind high or low spending. These include the size of the youth population, the rate of participation in programmes, the length of programmes and the annual cost per student. An alternative way of measuring the "effort" devoted by each country on education is to focus on the per-student costs, relative to GDP per capita. This second indicator can be interpreted as a measure of the average resources spent on educating each young person relative to a country's ability to pay. It is particularly relevant for stages of education at which participation is universal or near-universal.

Overall, about 6 per cent of GDP on average is spent on education and training, most by the public sector...

Figure 3.1 shows both the total proportion of GDP devoted to education and training, and the relative annual cost of a student at various educational stages. On average, OECD countries spend 6.3 per cent of GDP on education and training, of which four-fifths (5.2 per cent of GDP) is direct public expenditure on educational institutions. The reporting of private sources of expenditure (including families, individuals and businesses) varies across countries so that a direct comparison is not possible except for a limited set of countries. However, for those countries which provide comprehensive data on private sources of funding for both tuition and other costs associated with education, the total amount spent varies from around 1.8 per cent of total GDP in the United States to 0.8 per cent in France.

... but this total depends on a combination of factors...

Many of the countries with high overall spending relative to GDP (shown in part B, Figure 3.1) also have high spending per student (shown in part A). In particular, the Nordic countries have mainly high relative spending on both measures. In some cases the two indicators produce very different pictures. For example, Austria spends about twice as much educating a student in primary education, relative to GDP per capita, than does Ireland. However, overall, the two countries spend a similar percentage of national income on education and training. This situation arises in large part because Ireland has more than average, and Austria fewer than average, young people. A higher than average, proportion of young Irish people but a lower than average proportion of young Austrians are enrolled in education. These demographic and enrolment rate differences

◆ Figure 3.1. **Spending on education relative to national income, 1994**

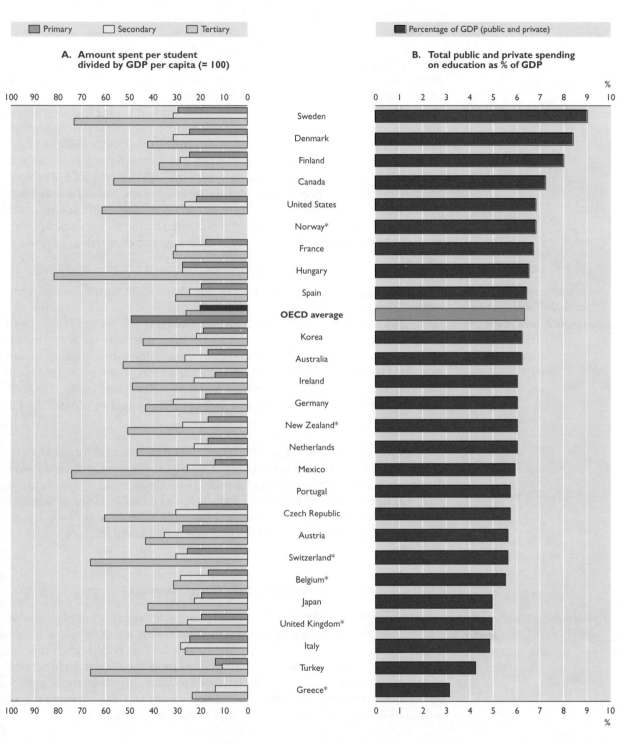

OECD countries devote a substantial proportion of their national income to education,
but the amount spent on each student varies greatly by educational level.

* Public sources only (Part B only).
Data for Figure 3.1, p. 103.
Source: OECD (1997c).

make Irish spending 1 per cent of GDP higher and Austrian spending 1 per cent of GDP lower than they would otherwise be: a substantial proportion of the total spent on education (see OECD, 1997*b*, p. 15).

As well as overall enrolment rates and unit costs, a number of other factors have an important effect on overall spending. These include differences in the distribution of enrolments between more or less expensive sectors and fields of study. In some countries, private payments other than to educational institutions (*e.g.* expenditure by households on student living expenses, books, and other supplies) are considerable, exceeding 0.5 per cent of GDP in Finland, the Netherlands, Norway, Spain, Sweden and Turkey (see OECD, 1997*c*, Indicator B1.1*a*). Government financial aid to students for living expenses is also substantial in many countries, ranging from below 0.05 per cent of GDP in Japan and the United States to over 1 per cent of GDP in Denmark, Norway and Sweden. The lower levels of public expenditure for formal education in countries such as Germany, Korea and Japan are partly explained by the high levels of private sources of funding (including company funding for the dual training system in Germany).

... a key variable is spending per student; countries vary greatly in the relative resourcing of students at different educational levels.

Spending per student relative to per capita GDP varies considerably, among both richer and poorer countries. On this measure, two countries with vastly different levels of per capita income (Hungary and Switzerland) spend similar portions of that income to educate the typical primary student. There is also variation in the relative amounts of expenditure per student across education levels. For example, in Italy, approximately similar amounts are spent per student across primary, secondary and tertiary levels, whereas in Ireland, over three and a half times as much is spent per student at tertiary than at primary level.

Indicators of spending on education over time are less robust than for current spending, because of relatively recent improvements in comparability. However, it should be noted that spending on education as a percentage of GDP has been relatively stable since the 1970s (see OECD, 1996*a*, Chapter 1). Rising rates of participation among young people have to some extent been offset by reductions in the size of the youth population and the containment of unit costs.

Expenditure on public labour market training programmes

Governments also invest in adult skills through labour market training programmes.

In addition to making the larger part of the investment in initial education and training, governments contribute to subsequent investments in human capital by adults. One strategic way of directing limited public funds towards direct enhancement of human capital is through programmes designed actively to assist employed and unemployed people to function in the labour market. Active labour market programmes include education and training programmes as well as temporary employment schemes and recruitment subsidies.

Public expenditures on labour market training programmes directed at the unemployed and other disadvantaged groups in the labour market, as well as on training of the employed, average 0.34 per cent of GDP. But as shown in Table 3.1, there is wide variation across countries, with some of the Nordic countries, particularly Denmark and Sweden, spending substantially more than the average. Outside the Nordic countries, public expenditures on training under active labour market policies are generally very limited: the average spending drops to 0.24 per cent of GDP when the four Nordic countries are excluded.[1] Although this spending is low relative to investment in initial education and training, it should be borne in mind that spending on all public employment services, including those that may contribute indirectly to human capital even though they do not include training, is somewhat higher – around 1 per cent of GDP on average.

Table 3.1. **Public expenditures on labour market training programmes in OECD countries, 1995**

	Public expenditures as a percentage of GDP				
	Training for unemployed adults	Training for employed adults	Measures for unemployed youth	Vocational rehabilitation for disabled	Total
Australia	0.14	0.01	0.03	0.03	0.21
Austria	0.12	–	0.01	0.03	0.16
Belgium	0.16	0.12	–	0.04	0.32
Canada	0.25	0.01	0.01	0.02	0.29
Czech Republic	0.01	–	0.01	–	0.02
Denmark	0.62	0.40	0.17	0.29	1.47
Finland	0.45	–	0.08	0.06	0.58
France	0.34	0.04	0.09	0.03	0.50
Germany	0.38	–	0.05	0.13	0.56
Greece	0.01	0.08	–	–	0.09
Hungary	0.13	–	–	–	0.13
Ireland	0.16	0.06	0.12	0.09	0.43
Italy (1992)	0.02	–	0.28	–	0.30
Japan	0.03	–	–	–	0.03
Luxembourg	0.02	–	0.05	–	0.07
Netherlands	0.16	–	0.06	–	0.22
New Zealand	0.33	–	0.02	0.01	0.36
Norway	0.23	–	0.08	0.29	0.61
Poland	0.02	–	0.02	–	0.04
Portugal	0.05	0.15	0.15	0.04	0.39
Spain	0.24	0.08	0.09	–	0.41
Sweden	0.50	0.02	0.11	0.08	0.70
Switzerland	0.07	–	–	0.15	0.22
United Kingdom	0.09	0.01	–	–	0.10
OECD average*	0.19	0.08	0.08	0.09	0.34

– Missing data.
Public expenditure for apprenticeship and related forms of general youth training are excluded from the above table as these are generally included under public expenditure for education in Table A3.1 in the Annex.
* OECD average is an unweighted mean of all countries (including those which did not report data).
Source: Annex to the *Employment Outlook* (OECD, 1997a).

Investments by firms and organisations

Investments by enterprises play an important part in overall investment in human capital. Like spending on public labour market programmes, they are largely directed towards the development of those skills and competences with economic value. But it is difficult to measure such investment accurately, largely because much of it is not reported in company accounts. Such under-reporting has implications not only for policy makers trying to get an accurate picture of overall human capital investment, but also for companies in planning their investment decisions. If employee development is treated as a cost together

It is hard to measure all of the investment made by enterprises in human capital, partly because they tend to under-report training but also because much of informal learning is unmeasurable...

with other current expenditure, rather than being reported as investment associated with the creation of return-yielding assets, there may be a tendency to under-invest. While some of this under-reporting might potentially be rectified, part of the difficulty is the large amount of informal training that occurs in modern workplaces – through structured coaching or mentoring organised by management or workers seeking advice and information relatively independently. Such informal learning can never be measured adequately, and may continue to account for an unquantified component in the growth in human capital stock.

Data on investment in enterprise-based training are available for 11 European countries from the *European Labour Cost Surveys*, and from a number of additional national surveys, as well as, in some countries, from establishment administrative records. However, there is a lack of comparability in many of the results arising out of different definitions, coverage and reference periods in relation to enterprise-based training. Improving comparability is a major challenge for the future.

Some descriptive data are available on what firms spend on education and training of their own personnel, as well as on the main patterns of participation across countries, sectors, and size of organisations. Important issues for study include determining what incentives influence the level of investment companies make in training, and to what extent workers are able to alternate between work and both periods of on-the-job-training or off-the-job training over their working life.

... on average, about 2 per cent of payroll costs are invested by companies in training.

Using data from different sources, estimates of expenditures by enterprises on training as a percentage of total labour costs are provided for some countries in Table 3.2. The data indicate that enterprises devote about 2 per cent of total labour costs to firm-based training. This appears low in comparison to the overall

Table 3.2. **Expenditure on vocational training as a percentage of total labour costs (different years)**

	Industry	Services
EUROSTAT Labour Cost Survey, 1992		
Belgium	0.2	0.3
Denmark	2.5	2.9
France	1.5	1.4
Germany (former Federal Republic)	1.4	–
Germany (new *Länder*)	2.5	–
Greece	0.3	0.2
Ireland	1.5	2.0
Luxembourg	0.3	0.6
Netherlands	0.8	0.6
Portugal	2.6	1.5
Spain	0.3	0.4
United Kingdom	1.6	1.8
Average for EU countries	1.3	1.2
Other sources:		
Australia (1996)	2.5	
United States (1996)	1.8	

Australia: Australian Bureau of Statistics, survey of employer expenditure on structured training over the period July-September, 1996.
United States: American Society for Training and Development (ASTD) estimate over all firm sizes.
Source: EUROSTAT (1997), *Labour Costs 1992, Principal results.*

public and private expenditure on education as a percentage of GDP. However, in many countries, companies also contribute to the formation of human capital through the payment of levies for vocational or apprenticeship training.

Investments by families on human capital

Families make a considerable investment in activities that can directly or indirectly influence the development of human capital in their children. This investment is not only financial. Parental investment of time and the fostering of learning attitudes and habits are important inputs to the creation of human capital. Outlays for cost of tuition, educational materials and other costs associated with formal education can have a direct impact. Other spending that influences the quality of children's lives can have an indirect effect, which cannot readily be quantified. Although the total cost of rearing children from birth to early adulthood is not exclusively related to human capital investment as defined in this report, it is noteworthy that the total of such spending far exceeds the cost of formal education – either to public authorities or families. A study by Haveman and Wolfe (1995) found that annual expenditure on children aged 0-18 accounted for almost 15 per cent of GDP in the United States in 1992. They found that the private costs associated with housing, feeding, clothing, health care and transporting, as well as the indirect costs represented by the forgone earnings of mothers accounted for two thirds of all expenditure on children – or approximately 10 per cent of GDP. Public costs included expenditure for education as well as a wide range of social expenditure specifically aimed at young people (including services for disadvantaged young people).

Family investment in human capital can be hard to separate out from the high overall level of spending on children...

Although there is no way of measuring the exact degree to which spending on families contributes to the creation of skills and competencies, some indicators give a partial picture. One example is the availability of computers in the home (see box).

...although the number of computers in homes is one indicator.

Information technology and informal learning

The use of home computers has increased significantly in recent years. A major purpose of personal computers is education and informal learning. Consequently, disparities in home ownership of computers may have considerable consequences for educational achievements.

Percentage of households with personal computers in 1995

Denmark*	32.0
Canada	28.8
Netherlands	27.0
United States	25.5
Germany	25.0
Belgium	21.0
United Kingdom	20.0
Ireland	18.0
Japan	15.6
France	14.3
Italy	14.0
Spain	12.0

* 1996 data.
Source: OECD (1997d), *Information Technology Outlook*, Table 5.1, p. 88.

3. TIME INVESTMENT: MEASURING PARTICIPATION

Another measure of investment is the expected number of years spent by young people in study.

Participation rates in formal education and adult education and training, together with measures of duration, are an indication of how much time individuals invest in developing human capital, as well as a reflection of the learning opportunities available.

Participation in initial formal education

Two indicators developed by the OECD summarise the level of participation of each country's population in formal education. The extent of initial education for young people can be encapsulated by the number of subsequent years of schooling expected by a 5 year old. An overlapping measure, concentrating on post-secondary experiences throughout the life-span, measures the expected number of years of tertiary education from age 17. Both of these measures are shown in Figure 3.2.

Estimates show firstly that the average years spent by a young person in education is fairly similar across OECD countries...

The average number of years of enrolment in formal education that a 5-year-old child can expect up to the age of 29 is based on the current enrolment rates by age. This average number of years is just over 15, and in most countries the variation is within the relatively narrow band of between 14 and 17 years. This measure differs from the estimated average number of years of schooling discussed in Chapter 2 since the latter relates to the years completed by today's adults, whereas schooling expectancy is based on the current enrolment rates of young people at various ages.

... but secondly, that the average amount of tertiary education received over the whole of people's lives varies more widely.

School expectancy includes participation in tertiary education provided it takes place before the age of 29. This is a broad measure, influenced by the age at which children start school, by the compulsory leaving age and by the rate at which young people participate beyond that age. A more focused measure, shown on the right hand side of the figure, looks only at the expected years of tertiary education, based on current rates of participation by adults over all ages from 17 onwards. This is effectively the product of the number of years spent on tertiary education courses and the proportion of the population who participate in them. Since participation in upper secondary education is tending towards 100 per cent in many countries, tertiary participation is becoming the most important discretionary element in formal education systems. As shown in the figure, there is a variation by a factor of two in the average number of years received, even when the four countries with particularly low totals are excluded.

Overall, school expectancy has increased since the mid-1980s, in many countries by more than a year (see OECD, 1997c, Indicator C1.2, p. 141). But such change may involve the development of new types of programmes and pathways, rather than just a prolonging of studies within existing patterns. School expectancy needs to be understood in the context of marked differences in the types of programme and content of learning over time and across countries.

Participation in continuing education and training

National data on adult training is not sufficiently comparable internationally...

Data comparing the rates at which adults participate in education and training, in comparable form across countries, are limited. A review of enterprise-related training concluded that "the gap between what is actually

◆ Figure 3.2. **Average expected years of formal education, 1995**

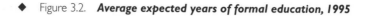

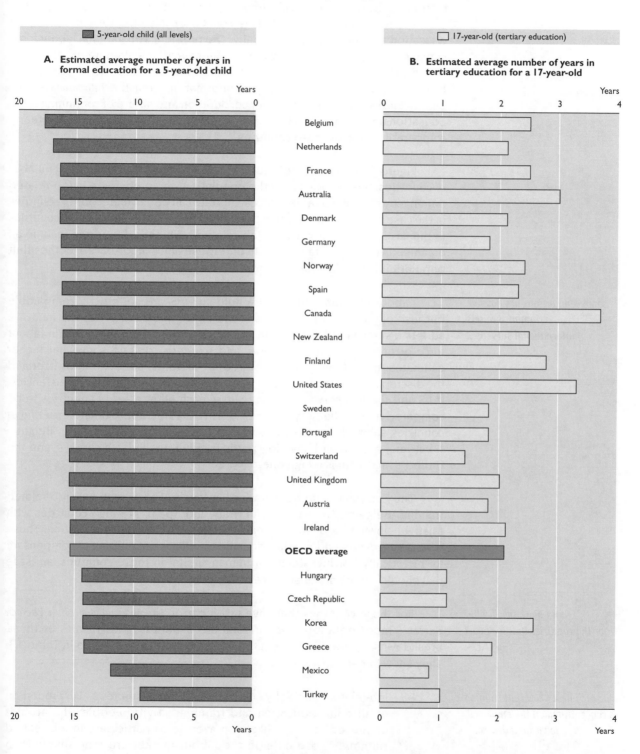

The years spent by young people in education is on average fairly similar across countries,
but the amount of tertiary education experienced in adulthood varies greatly.

Data for Figure 3.2, p. 104.
Source: OECD (1997c).

known about training on an international basis and what would be required in relation to the main analytical and policy questions is large" (see OECD, 1991, p. 161; see also OECD, 1993). This conclusion also applies to continuing education and training more generally. The problem with national labour force surveys and enterprise surveys, the main source of such data up to now, is that definitions of training and reference periods differ across countries. However, the recent availability of information from the *International Adult Literacy Survey* (IALS) on the incidence, duration and nature of continuing adult education and training in 11 OECD countries has provided more consistently comparable data for these countries.

Figure 3.3 shows the indicator that is available across the greatest number of countries: the percentage of the population who participate in job-related training. By combining three sources, this rate can be calculated for 14 countries in the case of participation within the preceding 12 months, and for 15 countries in the case of the past 4 weeks. Job-related training is defined to include all organised vocational training, both enterprise and school-based for the adult population (excluding full-time tertiary studies).

... some comparisons are possible through two sets of international surveys...

Labour force and other household surveys are not strictly comparable because of the differences in the scope of the questions. The IALS measure adopts a somewhat broader conception of training than that used in labour force or other household surveys, and so tends to yield somewhat higher estimates, notably in Canada in the United States, although in Switzerland the discrepancy is in the opposite direction. But despite these inconsistencies, IALS and the *European Labour Force Survey* each allow a set of countries to be compared in a similar way. It is noteworthy that the approximate ordering of countries shown by these two surveys is consistent. For example, Belgium (Flanders) and Ireland have low participation rates in both surveys, and the United Kingdom has a high one.

The European countries showing low levels of participation in job-related training, Belgium, Greece, Ireland, Italy and Spain, are also countries with relatively low levels of educational attainment in the adult population. These results suggest that adult education and training is not helping to compensate for historically low investment in human capital in these countries, an issue that should be of particular concern for policy makers.

... and more specifically, for the countries that took part in IALS.

For those countries that have taken part in the *International Adult Literacy Survey*,[2] more detailed comparisons are available. The results of these breakdowns reported in Table A3.5 in the Annex are summarised in Table 3.3. They show in particular that:

These show that training is concentrated on the employed, to varying degrees...

– Job-related training by employed people constitutes a high proportion of all adult education and training activity. People who are not employed[3] are less likely on average to participate in job-related training. Those outside the labour market are more likely than employed people to participate in education and training unrelated to work, but such activity involves a smaller proportion of the population than job-related training. These averages however disguise considerable variations. For example in the United Kingdom, adult education and training appear to be particularly work-oriented:

◆ Figure 3.3. ***Percentage participation by employed adults (aged 25-64) in job-related training, 1994-95***

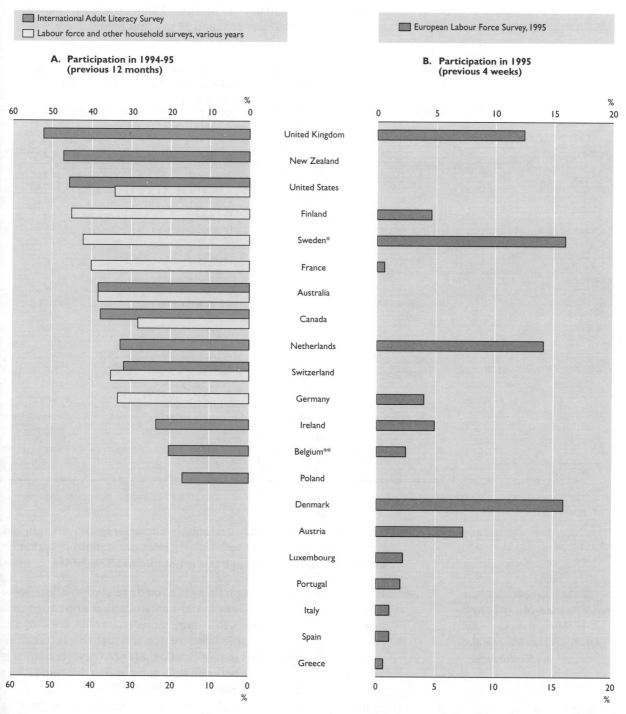

A. Participation in 1994-95 (previous 12 months)

B. Participation in 1995 (previous 4 weeks)

Between one in six and one in two employees participate in job-related training over a 12-month period.

*   Data from the LFS in Sweden relate to a six-month period (Part A).
** Belgium Flanders (IALS data only in Part A).
Data for Figure 3.3, p. 105.
Sources: International Adult Literacy Survey, OECD and European Labour Force Survey.

52 per cent of employed adults report having undertaken some work-related training over a 12-month period; in contrast only 7.3 per cent of adults outside the labour force report non job-related education or training. In Switzerland[4] on the other hand, these figures are more even, with rates of 32 per cent and 22 per cent respectively.

Table 3.3. **Participation in continuing education and training by adults: summary of results from the *International Adult Literacy Survey* in 1994-95**

Adults aged 25-64, past 12 months

Participation in:	by:	Unweighted country average (% of adults in each group)
a) Job-related training	Employed	34.4
	Unemployed	19.7
	Inactive	7.1
b) Other education and training (as main activity)	Employed	6.4
	Unemployed	6.0
	Inactive	10.6
Job-related training (gender breakdowns)[1]	Employed	
	Men	34.3
	Women	34.4
Job-related training (breakdowns by level of education)	Employed adults with:	
	Below upper secondary	20.2
	Upper secondary	34.0
	Tertiary education	49.4
Job-related training (breakdowns by age)	Employed adults aged:	
	25-34	37.7
	35-44	36.3
	45-64	29.7

Note: Respondents were asked about the main education or training activity that they undertook in the past 12 months.
Refer to Tables A3.5, A3.6 and A3.7 in the Annex.
1. Data on participation by gender are not shown in the Annex. In most countries, rates of participation in job-related training are similar for men and women.
Source: International Adult Literacy Survey.

... the better-educated train more than less-educated people in their own country – but not always than less-educated in other countries...

– The incidence of job-related training is similar for employed men and women. For the unemployed, training rates are somewhat higher on average for women, although this is not true in all countries.

– Participation in continuing training is strongly related to educational attainment. Those with less initial human capital appear to lack incentives or opportunities to acquire more in later life, creating the risk of exclusion. It is notable however that although this is true in all countries, the differences in participation rates between countries is as great as the differences between well- and poorly-educated groups within countries. So an employee in the United Kingdom with below upper-secondary education is more likely to participate in training than one with tertiary education in Belgium (Flanders), Ireland or Poland.

– There is a modest, but not extreme, difference in participation rates by age. Employees in their 30s and early 40s are about as likely to receive training as their younger colleagues, but those aged

45-64 somewhat less so. This result is not surprising, given that older adults have received on average less initial education, and people with more education tend to train more. These results highlight the need to evaluate the training needs of older workers – especially those vulnerable to unemployment.

The above indicators show whether or not people engage in education and training at least once during a given period. But participation can involve anything from a one-day course to studies lasting for a year or more. The IALS data also make it possible to consider the duration of training. Respondents were asked about the length of up to three training activities in which they were engaged. The total number of hours that each of them spent on these activities in the course of a year are shown in Figure 3.4 (and in Table A3.4 in the Annex), alongside participation rates. In some cases wider participation is associated with shorter courses, and *vice versa*. For example, of the countries shown, the United Kingdom has the highest proportion of employees undertaking training,

... the duration of training must also be considered: high rates of participation may be for relatively short periods.

◆ Figure 3.4. ***Average duration of job-related training undertaken by employed adults aged 25-64, 1994-95***

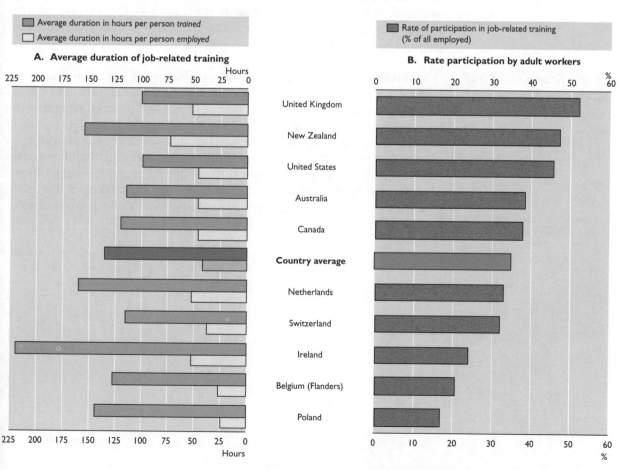

Average training per employee depends not just on the percentage being trained but also on the hours received by each.

Data for Figure 3.4, p. 106.
Source: International Adult Literacy Survey.

but the second lowest average hours per trainee. Ireland has less than half the participation rate of the United Kingdom but nearly double the hours per trainee. Australia has the most training hours per employee, because nearly half the population is being trained, and spends longer than average on courses.

4. CONCLUSIONS

The distribution of human capital investment beyond initial schooling does not appear well-matched to demand.

This chapter has shown that although OECD countries make investments of broadly the same magnitude in initial education, there are marked differences in both spending on, and participation in education and training across the life-span. In all countries, there is a concentration of such investment among younger, economically active, better educated people. Many groups who have greater need for training are in practice less likely to participate, increasing their vulnerability on the labour market.

The evidence also points to wide disparities in the intensity of different kinds of human capital investment. Funding levels differ greatly between levels of education and between formal and informal learning. The rationale for different levels of funding and mix of public and private funding *vis-à-vis* social and political objectives of governments is not always clear. The next chapter considers the evidence from existing data and research for evaluating the impact of investment and training in different settings.

More information is needed to fill in the picture of human capital investment.

The present chapter has, however, identified a number of important gaps in the data on investment in human capital. In particular, private expenditure for education and training is unevenly covered, and in some countries the coverage is extremely poor. It is therefore difficult to give a complete picture of how much total expenditure is devoted to different levels of education or training, not to mention the relationship between investment and outcomes for different actors. The chapter has also identified deficiencies and problems of comparability in international measurement of various types of continuing education and training. This gap in the knowledge base will be discussed further in Chapter 5.

INVESTMENT INDICATORS

Indicator	What it shows	Usefulness and limitations	Data availability and sources	References in this volume
a) Share of national income devoted to education and training.	Public and private expenditure on formal programmes, as a percentage of GDP.	Estimates overall resources devoted to investment. Excludes informal learning. Imperfectly compares national effort relative to need: countries with higher youth populations need to spend more.	Comprehensive data on public programmes available but limited availability of data on private spending.	Figure 3.1 and Table A3.1 in the Annex
b) Average spending per student, by educational level, relative to income per head.	Average annual expenditure on a student at primary, secondary and tertiary education, as a percentage of GDP per capita.	Shows how much effort is devoted to each student, relative to each country's means. Takes no account of variations in investment due to participation rates outside compulsory schooling.	As a).	Figure 3.1 and Table A3.1 in the Annex
c) Spending on public labour market programmes.	Expenditure as a percentage of GDP, classified by type of participant.	Shows direct expenditure by governments to improve workplace skills. Excludes some employment service spending relevant to human capital which is not strictly on training.	Data incomplete. See Annex to the *Employment Outlook* (OECD, 1997a).	Table 3.1
d) Spending by enterprises on training.	Expenditures as a percentage of total labour costs.	Gives rough a indication of the scale of spending by firms. But much private human resource investment is hidden.	Data from various surveys (including EU Labour Cost Survey) is incomplete, and not strictly comparable.	Table 3.2
e) Family computer ownership.	Percentage of households with personal computers.	Gives one indicator of a family-based resource that aids human capital investment.	Data for 12 countries provided in OECD (1997) *Information Technology Outlook.*	See box, p. 41
f) Expected years of schooling.	Average expected years of initial education for a 5-year old child to age 29.	Gives overall indicator of youth participation in education. Influenced by current participation rates.	*Education at a Glance – OECD Indicators* (OECD, 1997c).	Figure 3.2 and Table A3.2 in the Annex
g) Expected years of tertiary education	Average expected years of tertiary education from age 17 over a lifetime, based on headcounts of all adults currently participating.	Combines information on how many undertake tertiary education and the length of time they spend in it.	*Education at a Glance – OECD Indicators* (OECD, 1997c).	Figure 3.2 and Table A3.2 in the Annex
h) Employee participation in job-related training	Percentage who report having undertaken training in specified periods.	Gives a rough idea of the proportion involved in some kind of training, but does not distinguish length or quality. Data from different sources are not always comparable.	Several household, enterprise and administrative sources are available including the *International Adult Literacy Survey* and the *European Labour Force Survey.*	Figure 3.3 and Table A3.3 in the Annex

INVESTMENT INDICATORS *(continued)*

Indicator	What it shows	Usefulness and limitations	Data availability and sources	References in this volume
i) Participation by different groups in job-related and other education and training.	Breakdowns by economic status, age, gender, educational attainment.	Detailed comparisons for a limited number of countries.	*International Adult Literacy Survey.* Most breakdowns available for about 10 of the 12 countries. But for some categories (*e.g.* unemployed people), sample sizes limit validity of results.	Table A3.5 in Annex and summarised in Table 3.3
i) Average duration of job-related training.	Annual hours of training undertaken – *i)* per person with any training *ii)* average for all employees.	Qualifies indicator *h)* by showing quantity of investment rather than just the percentage of employees making some investment.	Hours of training available from IALS. *European Labour Force Survey* classifies participation by length of course.	Figure 3.4 and Table A3.4 in the Annex

NOTES

1.   In spite of rising unemployment, it is not clear that there has been a general tendency across countries to move from passive measures which provide financial supports for unemployed workers, to active measures designed to improve the skills and competencies of workers and support the search process in the labour market.

2.   Australia, Belgium (Flanders), Canada, Ireland, the Netherlands, New Zealand, Poland, Sweden, Switzerland (French and German speaking), the United Kingdom and the United States.

3.   It should be noted that due to sampling size, the averages and ranges for the unemployed and inactive populations in Table 3.3 are based on some figures that are not statistically significant.

4.   Excluding Italian-speaking cantons.

REFERENCES

EUROSTAT (1997), *Labour Costs, 1992, Principal Results*, Luxembourg.

HAVEMAN, R. and WOLFE, B. (1995), "The determinants of children's attainments: A review of methods and findings", *Journal of Economic Literature*, pp. 1829-1878, December.

OECD (1991), *Employment Outlook*, Paris.

OECD (1993), *Employment Outlook*, Paris.

OECD (1996a), *Education at a Glance – Analysis*, Paris.

OECD (1996b), *Education at a Glance – OECD Indicators*, Paris.

OECD (1997a), *Employment Outlook*, Paris.

OECD (1997b), *Education Policy Analysis*, Paris.

OECD (1997c), *Education at a Glance – OECD Indicators*, Paris.

OECD (1997d), *Information Technology Outlook*, Paris.

OECD, Human Resources Development Canada and Statistics Canada (1997), *Literacy Skills for the Knowledge Society – Further Results from the International Adult Literacy Survey*, Paris.

RETURNS TO INVESTMENT IN HUMAN CAPITAL

1. BENEFITS, COSTS AND RETURNS

Human capital investment confers benefits on individuals, enterprises and societies. These benefits may be economic in nature and accrue in the form of additional earnings, productivity or economic growth. Human capital investment can also give rise to a wide range of non-economic benefits including greater social cohesion, lower crime and better health.

The widespread acknowledgement of the benefits of education and other forms of learning should not lead governments and others to invest indiscriminately in human capital. In deploying finite resources, they need to know which forms of investment produce the best value for money. This calculation has to take account of the postponement of returns, often over long periods after the investment has been made. To calculate the economic return, the cost of investments should be examined alongside the value of future benefits – "discounted" to take account of their postponement. To compare alternative investments, this information can be combined to produce in each case an annual "rate of return".

The costs and benefits of alternative investments in human capital need to be compared...

The difficulty in calculating rates of return on human capital investments is that even though some of the costs can be identified (see Chapter 3 above), it is hard to attribute, quantify and value the benefits that result, for two main reasons. First, while average benefits to individuals in terms of increased earnings and employment prospects are often clear, it is not always as easy to quantify benefits to society – which are highly relevant given that the cost of the investment is often borne in large part by public money.

Second, it is easier to look at the relative prospects on average of a person with a particular level of initial education than to do the same according to further investment over the lifecyle, because such investment is more heterogeneous in its nature, and its benefits are less generalised. So, information on returns tends to be skewed towards the benefits of formal education and training. Such data neglect deletes one of the fundamental characteristics of human capital, discussed in Chapter 1 above – its progressive accumulation

... calculating returns is difficult, because collective benefits are hard to measure and individual benefits cannot readily be attributed to specific investments over the lifecycle.

over a lifetime. A company whose capital accounts looked only at its founding investment, and not at depreciation or subsequent investments, would report a highly inaccurate rate of return on capital employed.

This chapter reviews, in the following section, evidence of the benefits to investment in human capital. It starts with the easiest to measure benefit: the employment and earnings gain from higher levels of educational attainment. It then looks at new evidence comparing the importance of attainment in this respect relative to that of directly measured skills. What is more difficult is systematically to attribute economic benefits specifically to episodes of investment in such skills, for example through enterprise-based training or public labour market programmes, but dispersed evidence does exist. A further difficulty is moving from the benefits to individuals to collective or social benefits. Section 2 concludes by considering in turn economic benefits to whole nations and "spin-off" social impacts of human capital investment that can in turn have indirect economic effects. Here too, there is clear evidence of benefit, but difficulties in measurement that would make it hard to calculate accurately rates of return.

Section 3 looks at the limited ways in which investment costs and benefits can be drawn together to calculate rates of return. These relate only to investment in initial education, and are based largely on individual returns to public and private investments, although one kind of social benefit – enhanced tax revenues – can be taken into account.

2. EVIDENCE OF BENEFITS OF INVESTMENT IN HUMAN CAPITAL

Benefits to individuals of initial education and training

Individuals with more education have better employment and pay prospects...

Educational attainment is positively related to individual performance in the labour market. Those with higher levels of education are more likely to participate in the labour market, face lower risks of unemployment, and receive on average higher earnings.

Figure 4.1 shows two important indicators of how labour market experiences differ for people with different levels of education. Part A shows that more educated women are much more likely to be working during their 30s and early 40s than less educated ones. Part B shows that less educated adults of both sexes are likely to experience more than average unemployment over their lives.

... particularly among women with higher levels of education and in countries where average female participation in the labour force is low...

The rate at which women participate in employment is particularly important because of its wide variation among different countries and generations. The focus of the comparison is the population aged 30-44 years, a relatively narrow age band of adults, most of whom have completed full-time education, and who have more similar experiences of work than a wider age range.[1] Figure 4.1A shows, in particular, that women with tertiary education have a higher chance than other educational groups of being in employment. The gap tends to be the greatest in those countries where relatively few women on average are in paid employment – for example in Ireland, Spain and Turkey. In such countries, women who are tertiary graduates are about as likely to be in

◆ Figure 4.1A. ***Percentage of women aged 30-44 in employment, by level of educational attainment, 1995***

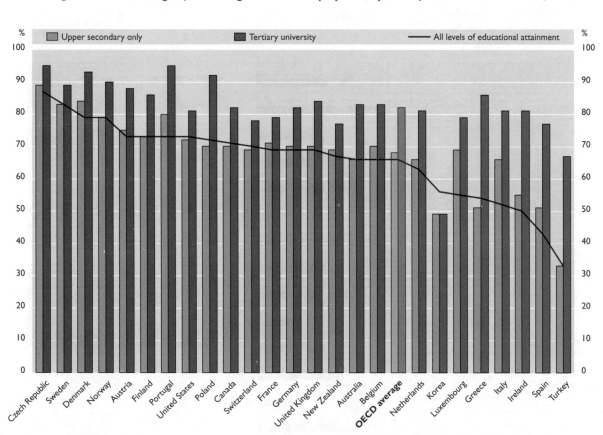

Countries are ranked by percentage for all educational levels combined.
Data for Figure 4.1A, p. 109.
Source: *Education Policy Analysis* (1997b), pp. 31 and 101.

In countries where fewer women work, those who are higher education graduates are much more likely than others to be in employment.

work as their counterparts elsewhere: the internationally low rates of participation are more pronounced for those with less education. Men's employment rates (not shown here) vary less, but still increase with educational attainment. In some cases the percentage of the least-educated men who are outside work at the prime of life is disturbingly high: at least 30 per cent of those aged 30-44 without upper secondary education are outside employment in Poland, the United States and the United Kingdom (see OECD, 1997a, Indicator E2.1b, p. 252).

The labour market effects of education need to be considered not just at one point in time, but also over the whole lifecycle. One telling indicator, shown in Figure 4.1B, is the average number of years an individual can expect to spend in unemployment over a working lifetime at different levels of education. This figure is calculated on the basis of actual unemployment rates among all age-groups in a single year, 1995. It is therefore indicative of the difference that education can make in unemployment expectation, rather than an accurate measure of an individual's expected time out of work, which depends *inter alia* on business cycle patterns.

◆ Figure 4.1B. *Expected years of unemployment over a working lifetime, by level of educational attainment for men aged 25-64, 1995*

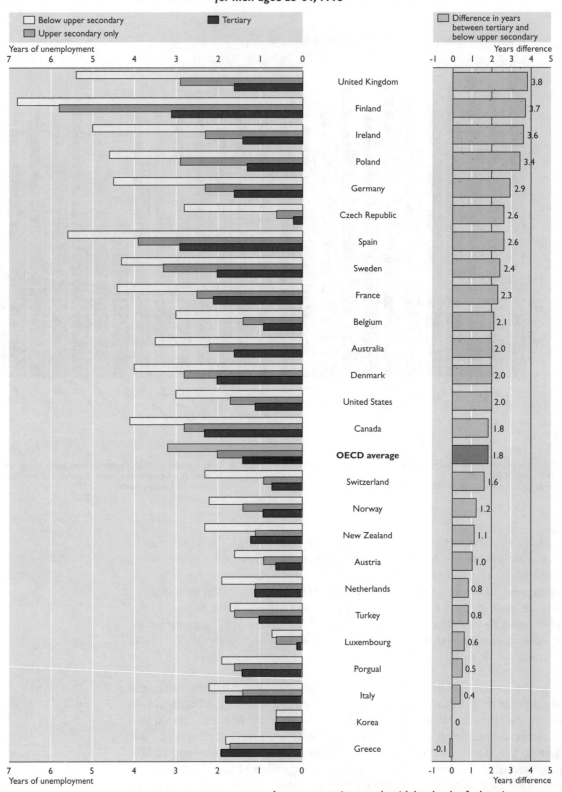

In some countries, people with low levels of education can expect to experience over three years more unemployment than the well educated.

Data for Figure 4.1B, p. 110.
Source: OECD (1997a).

On average across the countries shown, individuals with below upper secondary attainment can expect to spend more than twice as much time unemployed as tertiary graduates – 3.2 years rather than 1.4 years, in the course of a working life. This gap was greatest, in absolute terms, in countries with above-average unemployment in 1995 – for example in the United Kingdom, Finland, Ireland and Poland, where educational attainment made a three to four year difference in lifetime unemployment expectancy.

... better education on average more than halves expected years of unemployment over a working lifetime...

The scale of youth unemployment in many OECD countries constitutes a huge wastage of human potential for individuals as well as societies. Young people are particularly vulnerable immediately after leaving education: one year later, typically between one quarter and one half of those without upper secondary completion are unemployed (see OECD, 1997a, Indicator E6.1, p. 276). Those with more education tend to fare better, although in several countries unemployment rates are high for recent upper-secondary graduates, and in Spain about one half of tertiary-level graduates in 1994 were out of work a year later. However, the cost of inadequate investment in young people's human capital cannot just be measured in relation to the labour market. Associated problems of social exclusion, higher crime and poverty may carry even greater costs.

... with less-educated young people particularly vulnerable...

As well as being more likely to participate in the labour market, people with more education earn more on average over their lifetimes. This premium can be taken partly to represent a return on investment in human capital. However, earnings differentials by level of educational attainment are not determined purely by the more productive capacities of better-educated workers. They may also reflect a host of other factors including differences in the supply of educational programmes at different levels, barriers in access to those programmes, innate ability, provision for post-school training, unionisation and taxation rates.

Figure 4.2 shows relative earnings from employment for women and men in the 30-44 age group. By looking at earnings of the least- and most-educated groups relative to those who have just completed upper secondary education, the wage premium associated with completing each successive level of education can be seen. Those with less than upper secondary attainment tend to earn between 10 and 40 per cent less than those who complete upper secondary school. In general, men suffer a slightly smaller disadvantage than women as a result of not completing secondary education.[2] However, for both men and women, university education brings a higher premium: the gap in earnings between tertiary and upper secondary graduates is greater than the gap between those with and without upper secondary education. This may be because upper secondary completion has become the norm, and only those who rise above this norm attract big rewards. The university premium for women aged 30-44 years ranges from 20 per cent in Italy to 110 per cent in the United Kingdom. For men in the same age range, the premium ranges from 32 per cent in Switzerland to 80 per cent in France.

... the additional earnings associated with completing upper-secondary education is not as high as that for completion of tertiary education.

Benefits of acquiring measured skills

The evidence so far reviewed indicates a strong positive relationship, on average, between educational attainment and labour market outcomes. These positive effects of education are in many individual cases confounded, however, by differences in post-school experiences, by innate ability,[3] by family background and by other social factors. Studies that attempt to control for such underlying factors tend to find strong evidence of improved productivity,

Some critics maintain that education only confers benefits because it screens individuals for better jobs rather than by improving productivity...

57

◆ Figure 4.2. **Education and earnings of persons aged 30-44, 1995**
Mean earnings relative to upper secondary level only (100)

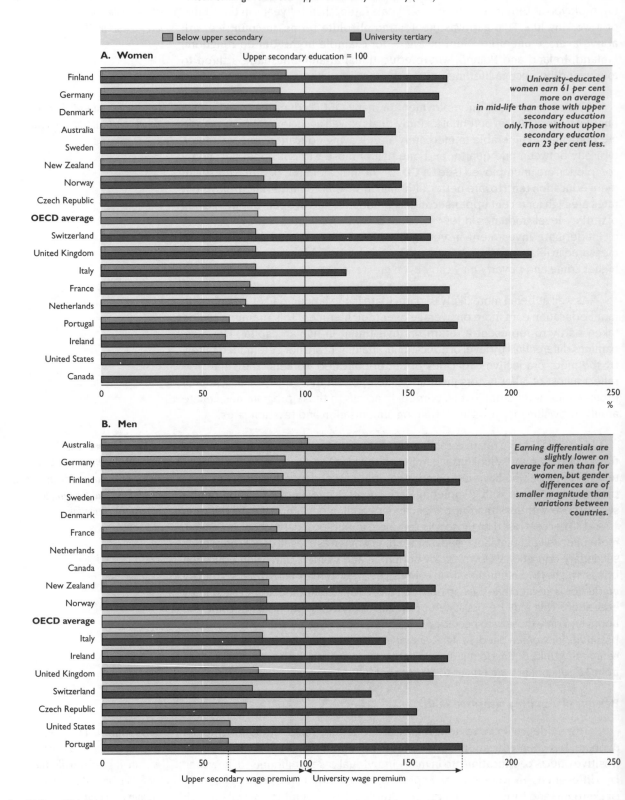

Data for Figure 4.2, p. 111.
Source: *Education Policy Analysis* (1997b), p. 33.

earnings and employment chances associated with both education and work-based training. However, a frequently asked question is whether these benefits are the direct result of education and training itself (through *investment* in skills and competences), or whether educational attainment acts mainly as a *screening* or sorting device that enables employers to allocate individuals to high-status or high-productivity occupations (Spence, 1974). If so, there is a risk that further expansion of learning opportunities would simply increase the supply of credentials and produce only limited social returns. To some extent, the *screening* and *investment* roles of education are not entirely incompatible. For example, employers may use educational qualifications as a signal of human capital – irrespective of how human capital has been formed (Groot and Hartog, 1995).

Recent empirical analysis (Altonji and Pierret, 1996) has examined how quickly employers learn about the true productivity of workers, and adjust their relative wages accordingly. This work suggests that the value of education in predicting future wages does not decline over time, because the increased information about individuals' productivity that employers acquire by observing them on the job confirms the expected relationship between productivity and education levels. Over time, they claim that the "signalling component" of educational qualifications accounts for a relatively small part of the wage differential associated with education.

Further research evidence (reviewed by Psacharopoulos, 1994) confirms that education appears to play a significant role in human capital formation, over and above any role it plays as a screening device. However, it shows that productivity-enhancing factors other than education and training play a parallel role. The results of the *International Adult Literacy Survey* (OECD, HRDC and Statistics Canada, 1997) give some indication of the relative importance of education compared to other factors, by providing evidence on the relationship between earnings, educational attainment and measured skills.

The IALS results show differences in gross earnings of individuals according to their literacy level,[4] their years of schooling and the length of their experience of the working world.[5] There are clear positive relationships between literacy, educational attainment and earnings. Table 4.1 presents estimates of the magnitude of the net direct effects of educational attainment, literacy scores and labour market scores on earnings. The coefficients indicate the strength of association between each factor and earnings. They suggest that educational attainment is in general more important than literacy in this respect. However, literacy does have a significant, independent effect: these calculations correct for the fact that someone with higher literacy is likely also to have more education and hence higher earnings. The independent effect of literacy varies considerably by country – in the United States, the United Kingdom and Ireland, it is about as great as that of education. In most other countries it is just over half as great, but in Poland it is negligible.

The International Adult Literacy Survey suggest that literacy significantly affects earnings both in connection with and separately from the effect of education.

The above results should be read with caution, as the precise relationship between education and the acquisition of the literacy skills tested in IALS is not sufficiently well understood. They do however indicate that, in some countries more than others, the acquisition of identifiable general skills influences lifetime pay prospects independently of one's educational qualifications. Conversely, the results confirm that many other factors are also at play in determining wage distributions. The final column of Table 4.1 shows that, typically, between one-fifth and one-third of earnings variation can be attributed to the combined effect of education, literacy and labour market experience.

Table 4.1. **Impact of educational attainment, literacy and labour market experience on earnings**

Table of regression coefficients

	Literacy[1]		Educational attainment[2]		Experience in the labour market[3]		Variance explained[4]
	Coefficient	se	Coefficient	se	Coefficient	se	R^2
Belgium (Flanders)	0.131	(.03)	0.484	(.04)	0.352	(.03)	0.413
Canada	0.197	(.03)	0.356	(.03)	0.242	(.03)	0.279
Germany[5]	0.189	(.03)	0.244	(.04)	0.116	(.04)	0.190
Ireland	0.309	(.04)	0.274	(.04)	0.232	(.03)	0.286
Netherlands	0.195	(.03)	0.272	(.03)	0.350	(.03)	0.260
Poland	0.003	(.03)	0.347	(.03)	0.176	(.03)	0.202
Sweden	0.103	(.03)	0.179	(.03)	0.265	(.03)	0.160
Switzerland[5, 6]	0.178	(.03)	0.304	(.03)	0.263	(.03)	0.225
United Kingdom	0.231	(.03)	0.243	(.03)	0.089	(.02)	0.232
United States	0.296	(.03)	0.302	(.03)	0.145	(.02)	0.333

Note: This table indicates the size of the direct effect of different variables on earnings using β coefficients. These coefficients are standardised maximum-likelihood regression estimates using LISREL path models while controlling for gender and parental education. The estimates minimise the error introduced by the presence of multi-collinearity between educational attainment and literacy.

se standard errors.

1. Literacy corresponds to measured literacy scores on prose, document and quantitative scales.
2. Educational attainment was measured by means of estimated years of schooling.
3. Work experience corresponds to the number of years since completion of formal education.
4. Percentage of total variation in earnings explained by literacy, educational attainment and experience combined.
5. Data refer to after-tax earnings in Germany and Switzerland.
6. Data are combined for the French- and German-speaking communities in Switzerland.

Source: International Adult Literacy Survey, 1994/95 (see OECD, Human Resources Development Canada and Statistics Canada, 1997, *Literacy Skills for the Knowledge Society – Further Results from the International Adult Literacy Survey*, pp. 45 and 165).

Benefits of enterprise-based investment in human capital

Enterprise-based training can produce gains to both individuals and firms, but they are difficult to measure...

Enterprises make substantial investments in the development of their workers in the hope that productive capacity will be enhanced. Most analysts agree that investment in training by enterprises is essential to increasing productivity and maintaining competitiveness. Gains from enterprise-based training can be looked at in terms both of the human capital held by individuals and the overall productivity of the enterprise. It can be difficult however to show direct links between particular episodes of investment and specific productivity gains, and harder still to aggregate the effects of such investments to calculate their overall effect on production or earnings.

An important reason for attempting such measurement is the danger of under-investment in training due to market failures. In particular, the fact that enterprises do not "own" the human capital embodied in their employees may deter them from investing in resources that can be poached by other firms. Other potential market failures arise from unequally distributed information on training, particularly in firms of differing size and in different sectors, and from imperfect capital markets to finance training. The evidence on market failure is not clear-cut, however. For example, two recent papers on training in France come to very different conclusions on the question of worker mobility following training.[6] Moreover, the common view that employers will only pay for firm-specific skills is challenged by a recent study showing that most of the skills learned in training are useful elsewhere (Loewentstein and Spletzer, 1997).

Table 4.2 provides a summary of the principal findings of the international literature on the benefits of enterprise-based training for individuals and firms. While it is difficult to generalise from such a diverse sample of studies, the weight of the empirical evidence is that:

... and dispersed evidence indicates that:

- training does generate *increased wages* for trained workers, and *increased productivity* for those enterprises that train and innovate. Some of the gain goes to workers in wages and some is kept by firms: it has been estimated that these two shares are of roughly the same size (OECD, 1994, Part II, p. 126);

... training does improves productivity, with about half the gain distributed in wages...

- enterprise-based training has the *greatest impact* on performance when undertaken in connection with changes in work organisation, job structure, and, in some instances, technological innovation (Black and Lynch, 1996; Ichniowski *et al.*, 1994).

... the impact is greatest in connection with change in work structures.

Benefits of public labour market training programmes

Public labour market training and other active programmes to enhance the employability of various types of worker have played an important part in government strategies to improve human capital (see Chapter 3 above). There has been increasing interest in research on their effectiveness.

The international literature suggests that the macroeconomic impact of such policies in creating additional employment is limited, with the exception of direct job-creation measures. However, training programmes may generate net employment gains under conditions of skill shortages or mismatches (Calmfors, 1994; OECD, 1993). Moreover, several studies show that spending on active labour market programmes can help lower unemployment, including its "structural" or long-term level (Scarpetta, 1996), and can help labour markets to adjust to sudden change.

The evidence of impact of public labour market training programmes shows some impact on unemployment...

At the *micro*-economic level, the potential contribution of such policies is to enhance employment opportunities for individuals belonging to less-advantaged labour market categories – whether at the expense of other individuals or because of the creation of new jobs. Here the empirical evidence is inconclusive. Table 4.3 provides a summary of studies of the impact of active labour market programmes, which are mainly concentrated in North America. Europe lags behind North America in the availability of good evaluations of active labour market policies which measure their effectiveness in improving employability and enhancing earnings.

... as well as benefits to some individuals but possibly at the expense of others...

Insofar as there is international evidence (see OECD, 1993; Fay, 1996), it indicates low or insignificant benefits from public labour market training programmes in a wide range of OECD countries. This evidence cannot be taken as conclusive, partly because few studies have been long enough in duration to measure adequately long-run effects, and because they do not typically account for spin-off social benefits like lower crime and better health. Moreover, training programmes that are targeted at specific client groups, that provide training in market-relevant skills, and that are adapted to individual skill needs have indeed been proved effective in enhancing employment prospects and earnings of their participants.

... well-targeted programmes providing market-relevant skills are more effective...

Table 4.2. **Impact of continuing education and training and enterprise flexibility on performance of workers and enterprises: summary of results from recent surveys and analyses**

Country and source	Findings
Canada, United States (Kling, 1995; Betcherman *et al.*, 1994)	New work organisation and specific work-place practices such as training, alternative pay systems, and employee involvement are often correlated with higher productivity. These and other practices are associated with greater productivity when implemented together. Gains in labour productivity and reductions in units costs are greater when work-place education programmes are present to support organisational change.
Canada (Human Resources Development Canada, 1996)	A major review of the impact of technological and organisational change concluded that the association between technology and firm performance is positive, but that effects on employment growth tend to be weaker. Bundles of organisational innovations, including training, can result in better performance. Technologically and organisationally innovative firms place a premium on highly skilled workers and tend to pay them more.
Canada (Betcherman *et al.*, 1997)	Wages were found to be higher for employees who had received workplace training, and employers found a positive association between training and economic performance, although the direction of causation between training and performance could not be reliably established.
Denmark (Danish Ministry of Business and Industry, 1996)	Enterprises that introduced process or production innovation accompanied by training were more likely than non-innovators to report, for the period 1990-92, growth in output (11 per cent vs. 4 per cent); growth in employment (3 per cent vs. 2 per cent); and growth in labour productivity (10 per cent vs. 4 per cent).
Denmark (Lund and Gjerding, 1996).	Value-added per full-time employee was 26 per cent higher in manufacturing firms that exhibited more flexible organisational approaches, including an emphasis on training, than in the least flexible firms.
France (Laulhé, 1990)	Survey of employees in 1985. Employees who received some employer-sponsored training were much less likely to go from employment to unemployment and more likely to experience occupational mobility.
France, Germany, Netherlands, United Kingdom (Mason *et al.*, 1994).	Detailed comparison of productivity, machinery, and skills in matched samples of biscuit manufacturing plants found that although capital equipment was roughly equivalent, quality-adjusted productivity in France and Netherlands was 25 per cent higher than in the UK, and that levels in Germany were 40 per cent higher than in UK. The relatively low productivity of UK plants was largely attributable to the lower levels of qualifications of UK workers and to less effective on-the-job training which resulted in a less flexible workforce.
Germany, Japan, United Kingdom (Carr, 1992)	This analysis compared changes between 1981-83 and 1989-90 in labour productivity in vehicle component manufacturing. Over this period, UK productivity relative to German productivity rose from 30-50 per cent to 65-70 per cent, in part due to improved industrial relations, fewer inflexible work practices, and less overmanning. Continued productivity differences between enterprises in the two countries were attributed to lack of management skills, and less systematic use of training in the UK. Lower productivity levels in UK. plants relative to Japanese plants were attributed in part to the fact that, though engineering graduates in Japan were less well-prepared than those in the UK, their performance improved once in work due to ongoing firm-based training, better social support within the companies, and rotation between production and non-production settings.
Ireland (Barrett and O'Connell, 1997)	A panel survey of 260 enterprises found that while investment in firm-specific training conducted in 1993 had no measurable impact on productivity, measured in 1995, investment in general training had a positive and significant effect on productivity over the same time-lag.
Netherlands (Groot, 1994)	Analysis of a survey of employers found that, on average, more training raised productivity by 12 per cent and wages by 16 per cent.
Sweden (Ottersten *et al.*, 1997)	Analysis of a panel data set for small firms shows that training yields long-run increases in labour demand and net reductions in costs.
United Kingdom (Groot and Oosterbeek, 1995)	Analysis of employee data from the 1991 British Household Panel Survey found that on-the-job training increased wages by 15 per cent.
United Kingdom, Germany (O'Mahoney, 1992);	Comparison of changes in productivity levels between 1960s-1980s, shows the UK-German gap narrowing. The author concludes that the narrowing of the gap will not continue because of lack of investment in human and physical capital and research and development.
United States (Russell *et al.*, 1985)	A survey of 62 outlets of a multinational retail company found a significant positive correlation between sales volume per employee, and the proportion of employees who received sales training, and with the employees' perceptions of how seriously training was taken by the company.
United States (Bartel, 1989)	Formal training has a positive effect on productivity, and the effect is larger when firms evaluate training programmes according to their impact on productivity.

Table 4.2. **Impact of continuing education and training and enterprise flexibility on performance of workers and enterprises: summary of results from recent surveys and analyses** *(cont.)*

Country and source	Findings
United States (Holzer *et al.*, 1993)	For a sample of manufacturing firms which applied for a state training grant, investment in training (measured as annual hours of training per employee) had a positive and significant impact on productivity (measured in terms of "scrappage rate", the proportion of output which could not be sold due to faults).
United States (Bishop, 1994)	On-the-job training has a positive impact on productivity and wage growth; a doubling of length of training raises productivity by up to 5 per cent, but raises wages by only 1 per cent.
United States (Ichniowski *et al.*, 1994)	In steel finishing plants, high-performance work practices (problem-solving teams, profit-sharing plans, pay for knowledge, formal training) have a significant positive effect on productivity, particularly if they are used together.
United States (Black and Lynch, 1996)	A survey of 3 358 establishments found that there are strong links between new work practices and the incidence and depth of training, that there are strong comlementarities between training and investments in both human and physical capital, and that investments in human capital have positive effects on productivity.

The evidence also suggests that the content, duration and certification of training are important issues. The modest benefits that arise are often in line with the modest scale of the programmes. Given that the amount invested is relatively low per participant, to expect it to raise future earnings by a large amount would imply an extremely large and implausible rate of return. Where labour market programmes help raise annual earnings, they do not in general do so by helping participants into higher quality, better paid jobs, but rather by increasing the number of hours worked per year (Fay, 1996). The effectiveness of such programmes therefore depends more on how they are targeted and designed around the immediate circumstances of their participants than on whether they are related to longer and more formal types of education or training.

... content, duration and certification of training are important issues.

Macroeconomic benefits to nations

The impact of education and training on macroeconomic performance has been the subject of considerable analysis and measurement over recent decades. Attempts to identify the precise contribution made by human capital to growth has spawned more theories than agreed conclusions. The history of these theories and associated attempts at measurement is summarised in the box.

The debate revolves around the respective roles of various "inputs" in contributing to growth. In particular, the theories try in various ways to separate out the contributions of the quantity of physical capital, the quantity of labour, the quality of labour, defined for example by the average educational level of the population, and the technological capacity of the economy. An underlying difficulty is that it can be hard to disentangle the impact of these last two factors, since the characteristics of workers closely interact with the technological or organisational environment in which they work. The balance of evidence indicates that both human capital and technological know-how are vitally important in growth. The evidence also indicates that this effect is not homogeneous, so strategies for investing in education, training and know-how need to be highly discerning if the desired impact on growth is to be realised.

There has been much debate and analysis about human capital's contribution to economic growth.

Table 4.3. **Selected evaluations of the effectiveness of labour market training and employment programmes**

Country and source	Findings
Canada (Abt Associates, 1993)	Quasi-experimental evaluation of a range of programmes for the long-term unemployed, young labour market entrants and women re-entrants. Mostly insignificant long-run effects of general training, although the effects of job-subsidies for the long term unemployed and work experience for young entrants and women re-entrants were positive and significant in the long-run.
Canada (Human Resources Development Canada, 1995)	Quasi-experimental evaluation of Employability Improvement Programme found significant effects on both employment duration and earnings for job-related training programmes.
Denmark (Jensen et al., 1990)	Analysis of training programmes mainly directed at low-skill manual labour market based on public registers in the Danish Longitudinal Database. Effects on wages are small, although for those with good initial employment conditions, the wage effect is positive and significant, while for those with high initial unemployment the wage effect is negative. Initial employment conditions has similar effects on subsequent unemployment.
Ireland (O'Connell and McGinnity, 1997)	Analysis of the impact of a range of differing training and employment programmes on offer in Ireland in 1992, based on follow-up surveys of both programme participants and a comparison group of non-participants. Both training and employment programmes with strong linkages to the open labour market have positive and significant effects on subsequent employment probabilities and wages, while programmes with weak market linkages have no measurable impact.
Norway (Raaum et al., 1995)	Quasi-experimental analysis of labour market training programmes. Found significant positive effects of training leading to formal qualifications leading to employment in particular economic sectors.
United Kingdom (Payne et al., 1996)	Quasi-experimental analysis of Employment Training (ET) and Employment Action (EA – a direct job creation scheme) found that training in ET had a significant effect of employment probability, while EA had no significant effect. Training combined with job placement had a further positive effect.
United States (Bassi, 1984)	Analysis of longitudinal data on participants in the Comprehensive Employment and Training Act Programme (CETA). The benefit from training for women is substantial, but no significant findings for men. This study also found evidence of non-random selection or "creaming off" of "less hard-to-place" candidates for programme participation.
United States (Card and Sullivan, 1988)	Study of a cohort of male participants in CETA. Positive effects on employment probabilities in the three years following the programme for participants in both classroom and on-the-job training programmes.
United States (Bloom, 1994)	Experimental random assignment study of classroom training under the Job Training Partnership Act found no significant impact of training on wages.
United States (Jacobson et al., 1994)	Longitudinal analysis of classroom training offered to displaced workers in Pennsylvania in the mid-1980s. Significant positive effects on earnings about 18 to 30 months after completing training. Training combined with job-search assistance also had a significant impact for men.
United States (Decker and Corson, 1995)	Analysis of two nationally representative samples of participants in training for displaced workers in 1988 found no significant effects of any impact of training on earnings, even though the programme was well-targeted on workers who had been permanently displaced from their jobs and had experienced significant earnings losses due to their layoff.
Sweden (Tanás et al., 1995)	Quasi-experimental analysis of wage gains found differentiating effects, with 1992 graduates experiencing (non-significant) wage losses and 1994 graduates experiencing significant wage gains of the order of about 3 per cent, compared with control groups over a 6 month period.

Research, technical know-how and innovation impact on growth and not just education on its own.

Models that give undue weight to educational attainment as a motor of growth have been vulnerable to criticism by those who see education as a way of allocating jobs through "screening" (Spence, 1974). Moreover, differences in income by educational attainment can partially be explained by the correlation of attainment with innate ability (Denison, 1964), and so do not guarantee that higher overall attainment will contribute to growth. So, some new growth theories have tried to build a more complex model accounting for human capital formation. Not just education itself, but its by-products such as research and innovation are given prime importance, as are internally generated technical

Human capital and economic growth: four decades of economic debate

Since the 1960s, economists have been seeking to account for the growth in aggregate output by looking at the rate at which various inputs are growing. The starting point of many economists (Denison, 1962) was that output had grown faster than would be implied by the rate of expansion of the two main economic inputs, capital and labour. This unaccounted-for growth was attributed to a "residual" factor, assumed to represent technical progress or the "quality of labour". Early models of growth accounting found this factor to be large, but were unable to say precisely what it consisted of, as it was simply calculated as the difference between observed output growth and the growth in measurable inputs. More recent approaches have sought to explain more precisely the contribution of inputs such as labour quality and technical know-how, by building measures of these inputs into growth models and testing whether this reduces the residual or unknown factor.

The most common approximation for quality of labour has been educational attainment. A large literature developed in the 1960s and 1970s showed that at least some of the residual explanation for growth might be accounted for by using educational attainment as a proxy for labour quality: in the United States, it could explain additional growth of about 0.5 per cent per year, or one-third of the calculated residual, according to one study (Jorgenson and Griliches, 1967). However, more recent work has shown that such effects may not be universal. A major study that tracked growth in seven OECD countries over four decades (Barro and Sala-i-Martin, 1995) found that growth in labour input,[*] even adjusted for educational attainment, made almost no net contribution to output growth in the four European countries involved. In the case of these countries, increases in both educational attainment and total number of persons employed were partly offset by reductions in hours worked per person. In Japan, Canada and the United States the labour contribution was higher – for example accounting for over 40 per cent of growth in the US between 1967 and 1989.

---

[*] Defined as the product of number of persons employed, hours worked per person and an index of educational attainment.

change, increasing returns to scale, the know-how acquired in the course of technology-intensive production and the spillover effect of a growing, "leading-edge" export sector on knowledge throughout the economy.

Recent studies have therefore tested the relative importance of educational and non-educational factors. Even though they have not produced a single new theory, some interesting results have emerged. For example:

- The marginal impact of increases in various levels of education appears to vary greatly according to the state of a country's development. A study by Mingat and Tan (1996) for the World Bank found that the level of higher education is most important in high-income countries, and primary education levels are a significant motor of growth in developing countries. While this result is not surprising, it confirms the possibility that over time, the expansion of any one level of education may yield diminishing returns.

- There is a strong identifiable relationship between human capital growth and the growth not just in output but also in labour productivity. This relationship is however strongest when comparing less and more developed countries (Lau *et al.*, 1991) than when comparing OECD countries, where it is obscured by the importance of other factors. Nevertheless, a study by Englander and Gurney (1994) looking simultaneously at the effect on productivity of growth in the capital to labour ratio, the size of the labour force and the enrolment rate in secondary education found that the latter had contributed 0.6 per cent to annual productivity growth in OECD countries between 1960 and 1985.

– When spending on research and development is included in the model, the independent effect of human capital appears to be reduced. Nonneman and Vanhoudt (1996) used R&D spending relative to GDP as an approximation for technological know-how, adding it to an earlier model (Mankiw *et al.*, 1992). They found that some of the attribution of growth to education was instead associated with R&D spending.

The balance of evidence suggests a positive impact of human capital invest on economic growth...

The evidence of additional economic output attributable to education needs to be set against the cost of the investment. Mingat and Tan (1996) have attempted to use estimates of costs and benefits to calculate a "social" rate of return to education. On the basis of economic growth performance, they have calculated that the estimated "social" rate of return was well over 10 per cent per year in the case of tertiary education between 1960 and 1995 in OECD countries. If such estimates prove robust, they will provide important confirmation that investment is paying off for whole economies and not just for individuals.

Social benefits

... as well as through spin-off social effects, which can in turn have economic benefit.

Not all benefits of investment in human capital can be captured in terms of direct economic impact. The creation of knowledge, skills, competences and aptitudes relevant to economic activity affect not only performance at work but also social behaviour. "Spin-off" benefits may affect public health, crime, the environment, parenting, political and community participation and social cohesion, which in turn feed back into economic well-being.

Behrman and Stacey (1997) survey the results of different studies examining the relationship between education and some of the above variables. Unfortunately, most of the evidence relates to North America. There is therefore a need to extend this research to other countries as well as to improve the quality and coverage of information and data.

Health outcomes of education

Education is shown to be linked to health, in terms of:

There is clear evidence that better educated people tend to be healthier even correcting for the health benefits that they enjoy because of their higher income. Studies have shown that:

... better health outcomes for adults with more schooling...

– Adults with more schooling have generally better health outcomes on average. Taubman and Rosen (1982), using US data, show that schooling is negatively related to mortality while controlling for other factors. Evidence from Grossman (1975) using US data on high-income earners, and from Desai (1987) using data on low-income earners shows that schooling has a positive effect on health after controlling for other variables. Desai shows that more schooling reduces loss of working time through sickness after controlling for initial health status.[7] Rosenzweig and Schultz (1991) found that parents' level of schooling had a positive and statistically significant effect on birth weight of their offspring. Data regularly published by the US Department of Health show that persons with lower education levels tend to have poorer health, higher rates of disability days, and higher hospital utilisation (National Center for Health Statistics, 1996). Finally, work by Grossman and Kaestner (1996) shows that health levels, whether measured by mortality rates, morbidity rates, self-evaluation of health status or physiological indicators of health, are closely related to levels of educational attainment.

–   One reason for this association is the way people handle knowledge of health-related information. The above studies and others suggest that the better educated can process more information about health risks than the less well-educated – even controlling for different social and economic circumstances of individuals.

... better handling of health information by the more-educated...

–   For men at least, the independent effect of education on mortality appears to have grown over time. Feldman *et al.* (1989) analysed changes in mortality rates by level of educational attainment in the United States for white middle-aged men and women between 1960 and 1971-84. Among men, there was little difference in mortality by level of educational attainment in 1960, but mortality for better educated men declined rapidly in the 1971-84 period, leading to substantial educational differences by the later period. Among women, mortality declined for all educational levels, although it continued to be higher for the least educated. It is argued that trends in educational differentials for heart disease are responsible for much of the observed changes – the least educated are at substantially higher risk of death from heart disease than their better-educated counterparts. A correlation between long-term unemployment and health status was also found.

... particularly significant improvement in health outcomes for better-educated men...

The effect of education on health differs in countries at various stages of development. A cross-country estimation of human capital stock by the World Bank (Nehru *et al.*, 1993) found that estimates of human capital stock in 1987 were negatively correlated with indicators such as the fertility rate and infant mortality. The strength of these correlations was higher for middle to lower-income countries. But for richer countries, the strongest evidence of an education effect is on other health indicators, for example premature death of middle-aged men from heart disease.

... but different types of advantage in countries at various stages of development.

Crime and education

Research findings reported by Behrman and Stacey (1997) also tend to support the view that the major crime-reducing effects of education come not only from higher levels of educational attainment, but also from the socialising and supervisory activities of educational programmes. Reducing early school drop-out and failure may contribute significantly to avoiding crime and anti-social behaviour amongst young people. Studies in the United States of the long-term effects of early childhood programmes reviewed by Barnett (1995) indicate that such programmes can produce long-term effects on school achievement, grade retention and social adjustment. However, Barnett claims

Education appears to lessen the risk of crime through helping to socialise young people who remain in school...

that the effects depend on programme quality and that well-designed and intensive interventions are more effective than ordinary child-care. For children that are at risk, early childhood education programmes may be particularly effective. The social benefits of interventions to discourage early school drop-out may far outweigh the cost of such interventions. However, further research is needed to identify interventions that are most effective, and to quantify some of the social and individual benefits of early childhood programmes, not just in the United States where such research is more advanced, but in other OECD countries as well.

Education and teenage pregnancy

A study by Zill (1994) showed that in the United States, the incidence of teenage childbearing is 12 percentage points higher among teenage girls whose parents have less than upper secondary education than among those who have completed high school but not tertiary level education (see Behrman and Stacey, 1997, p. 141). Teenage parents have increased probabilities of dropping out of school and demonstrate lower parenting skills, and experience higher rates of poverty, especially if they have out-of-wedlock births.

... but the extent to which these benefits are linked to the knowledge and skills acquired through education has not yet been measured.

There is thus a body of evidence demonstrating associations between educational attainment and a wide range of positive social outcomes. Ascertaining the causal impact of education as opposed to establishing statistical associations of education with various outcomes is difficult. Education may generate effects in three ways: by changing individuals' preferences, by changing the constraints that individuals face, or by augmenting the knowledge or information on which individuals base their behaviour. Further research is needed to examine the ways in which education interacts with other factors including family background and parental preferences for the future to bring about better health and lower crime.

3. CALCULATING RATES OF RETURN

Most evidence on rates of return relates to individual benefits in additional earnings from employment associated with more education...

Describing examples of benefits of investment in human capital does not in itself show that this investment is worthwhile. In competing for scarce capital resources, investment projects need to demonstrate an adequate rate of return. Calculating such a rate requires consistent data on both cost and benefit streams. Although some general estimates can be been made of the rate of return on education to society (see box above), the main evidence derives from the higher earnings that accrue to individuals from formal education, relative to its cost.

... but it is possible in principle to calculate:

The public and private returns that accrue from education have been estimated using the indicators summarised in Figure 4.3. In all cases an annual rate of return is calculated on the basis of the cost of investment and the value of subsequent benefits, discounted to take account of their postponement.

... private returns, reflecting only private costs and before-tax earnings...

– The *private* return to education takes account only of privately borne costs (including foregone earnings) and private gains in terms of higher post-tax earnings.

◆ Figure 4.3. **Costs and benefits of human capital investment**

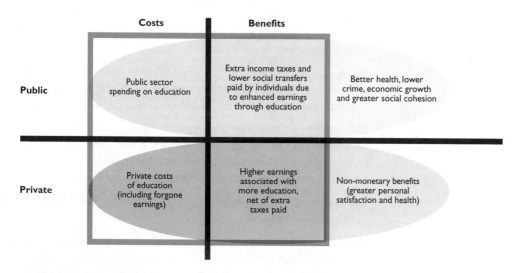

Source: OECD.

"Social" return includes all the items in the diagram, but in practice those elements within the square have proven the most amenable to measurement.

– The *"social"* return to education includes both private and public costs. By looking at gross earnings, it includes one element of public benefit – the higher income tax revenues paid by people who earn more as a result of their education. However, macroeconomic and wider social gains have not yet been built into calculations of these returns.

... "social" returns, narrowly defined, which consider both the public and the private side...

– The *fiscal* return to education looks at the direct implications for the public purse. It compares public costs to extra tax revenues and gains from lower payments of public transfers to those who require them less as a result of being more educated. This last benefit is difficult to measure accurately, and has not been used in calculating social returns; estimates of fiscal returns are as a result less reliable.

... and fiscal returns which relate only to additional tax receipts and lower social transfers for governments.

The private rate of return influences whether individuals decide to undertake education. The social rate of return influences whether societies collectively decide to finance education, by voting for taxes and making private contributions. The fiscal rate of return potentially shows governments the extent to which the public expenditure devoted to education will be recouped in long-run benefits to the public purse.

Data from the OECD's INES project (on international indicators of education systems) makes it possible to estimate social rates of return in different levels of education. The results shown in Figure 4.4 suggest that annual rates of return for upper secondary level are generally high (typically above 10 per cent) for both men and women. They are particularly high for women and men in Ireland, the Netherlands, Switzerland and the United States. Rates of return on tertiary education tend to be lower on average than rates on upper secondary.[8] In the case of seven countries, the rates for university education fall below 10 per cent for women, with particularly low returns in Italy, Sweden and Switzerland.

Returns appear to be particularly high for upper secondary, and somewhat lower for tertiary education...

... but these estimates have important limitations.

The data used for Figure 4.4 provide an overall indication of broad orders of magnitude, but cannot be treated as precise estimates because:

–   It takes no account of broader social or economic benefits flowing from investment in education.

–   It takes account of additional earnings arising from education for those in employment, but not of lower risk of unemployment arising from educational attainment, or other social and personal benefits.

–   Differences in earnings and employment by level of educational attainment in the course of a working lifetime compound differences in retirement incomes for different educational groups – these are not included in the estimate of lifetime returns.

–   Estimates of returns are sensitive to assumptions about forgone earnings of students.

–   The effects of various underlying assumptions in arriving at the estimates of rates of return may be open to question. For example, lifetime earnings across different age-groups at one point in time are not necessarily a reliable guide to the likely future earnings profile of a cohort graduating at a particular level of education today.

–   Between-country differences in estimated rates of return are strongly influenced by the overall earnings distribution in each country, which is determined by institutional and non-market factors as well as by those associated with human capital (see OECD, 1997b, Chapter 2).

–   Rates of return estimates are based on average earnings and costs. In practice there can be considerable variation in rates of return for different fields of study or particular social groups. So it should be emphasised that these rates of return are more relevant for governments thinking at the macro level about how to structure investments than for individuals making specific decisions about whether to study.

It is nevertheless interesting to make three observations about the broad orders of magnitude of estimated social returns to education, based on these and other calculations. First, they compare favourably with rates of return on physical capital. Second, although tertiary education yields greater marginal benefit in additional earnings than in the case of upper secondary level, it does not necessarily bring a better social rate of return. Third, rates of return have changed significantly over time.

Human capital seems to offer rates of return comparable to those available for business capital...

Published OECD data (see OECD, 1997c, Annex Table 25) on returns to business capital (including housing) indicate a return of around 16 per cent in 1995 across OECD countries on average (or 13.6 per cent in the case of the countries shown in Figure 4.4 and Table A4.4 in the Annex). Figure 4.4 shows returns to business capital alongside the estimates of returns to different levels of education. Returns to investment in upper secondary education tend on average to be at the level of returns to business capital, while returns on tertiary level education tend to be slightly less. However, the differences are relatively small. Mc Mahon (1991) has estimated the rate of return to human, physical and housing capital for the United States over the period 1967-87. He finds that, even in the absence of measures of externalities (including lower crime, better

◆ Figure 4.4. **Annual rates of return to education**
Estimated at different levels over a working lifetime in respect of employed persons only, 1995

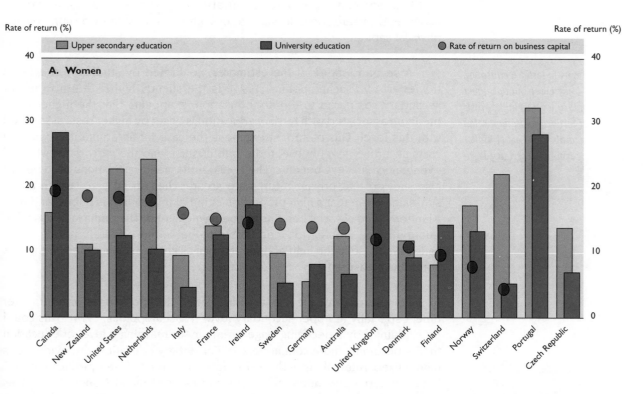

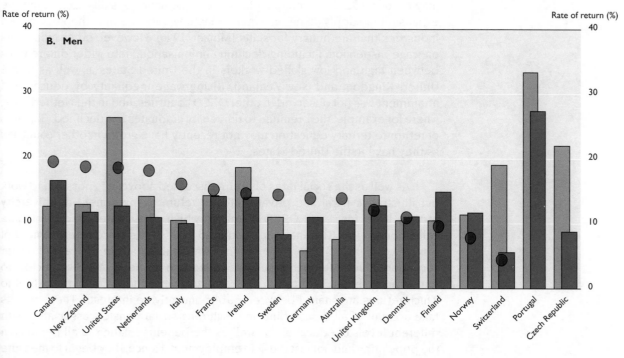

Countries are ranked by the rate of return on business capital.
Data for Figure 4.4, p. 113.
Source: Education Policy Analysis (OECD, 1997b), p. 35.

Rates of return at upper secondary level compare well to returns on business capital.
For university tertiary education, rates tend to be somewhat lower.

health, greater social cohesion, and research and knowledge in the case of higher education) and non-monetary returns,[9] rates of return on education (in the region of 10-15 per cent) compare favourably with those on housing capital (4 per cent) and are about the same as or slightly less than those on non-housing physical capital.

... returns to tertiary education tend to be lower than at upper secondary level as higher costs of tertiary education weigh againts the effect of higher earnings at tertiary level.

A second feature of the estimates, confirmed by studies in the 1980s (reviewed by Psacharopolous, 1994), is the slightly higher return to upper secondary compared to tertiary education. It appears that the higher wage premium associated with tertiary education is offset by higher costs associated with this level. This pattern strengthens the case for an equitable sharing of costs at tertiary level between the public purse and the individuals who will eventually reap large benefits. The 1980s studies (and calculations cited below) also showed that private returns are greater than social ones, which is not surprising given that a high proportion of initial investment is public, and only a limited range of social benefits are being measured. The prima facie case that this evidence creates for more costs to be borne privately needs to be considered also in the light of benefits such as greater social cohesion that are not being measured.

Long-term evidence seems to indicate a decline in rates of return over time, especially at upper secondary level (Psacharopolous, 1994). This could be explained by a declining wage premium for reaching a level of education that is becoming more commonplace. For tertiary education, the evidence is more mixed. After falling in the 1970s, rates of return to tertiary education rose in the United States during the 1980s and early 1990s (McMahon, 1991). This may be because of a continuing increase in demand for skills, exceeding the expansion of supply, in an era when many new jobs are in technology-based industries that are hungry for skills (Mincer, 1996). However, other influences on wage dispersion, including declining unionisation, help wider differentials between high and low skilled workers in the United States as well as in the United Kingdom and New Zealand. Rising wage inequality by educational attainment was not observed in other OECD countries, and in the Netherlands, where for example, the premium to university graduates has declined. So, rates of return to tertiary education may not recently have grown in other countries as they have in the United States.

As well as the social rates of return discussed above, it is possible to work out illustrative fiscal and private rates of return to investment at university tertiary level for seven OECD countries which participated in a pilot data collection in 1997. The analysis is confined to this level since measurement of private costs including forgone earnings was problematic in the case of upper secondary level. Although results calculated so far need to be subjected to further analysis and verification, they start to give an indication of the extent to which returns are shared between public and private interests. These results take account of all types of income including social transfers associated with different levels of education, as well as the benefits relating to all persons in the population and not just those in employment. Hence, they begin to measure the impact of unemployment or exclusion from the labour market in estimating lifetime benefits. In estimating lifetime benefits, it is assumed that income will grow over time by a constant 1 per cent per annum for all groups in the population.

The results of these experimental calculations are presented in Table A4.3 in the annex. They indicate that in the countries examined, there are positive fiscal and private returns to investing in University-level education. The private returns tend to be higher than the fiscal returns. The estimate of private returns indicates that in Australia, Canada and France, there are private returns in the region of 15-25 per cent for both men and women. For the other four countries (Belgium, Denmark, Sweden and the United States), the returns appear to be somewhat lower – notwithstanding the high relative premium in gross earnings for these countries at the university level.

Private returns appear to be higher than fiscal returns at university tertiary level...

In tertiary education, the sharing of costs is not closely related to consideration of rates of return: subsidies to households and institutions tend to be undifferentiated. One alternative approach to the sharing of costs is the taxing of private benefits from investment largely financed by the public purse. Further analysis would be needed to distinguish the effects of taxes on different types of educational programmes or learning, and to examine the impact of taxation on human as opposed to physical capital. Liebfritz *et al.* (1997) argue that in most OECD countries, corporate tax regimes generally favour intangible investment (including human capital) relative to physical capital, in that expenditures on such factors as education and training, and research and development receive relatively more favourable tax treatment than investment in plant and equipment. However, others have argued that tax regimes tend to work in the opposite direction (Miller and Pincus, 1998). The reduction in income tax progressivity in some OECD countries in the recent decade may have encouraged human capital formation at the tertiary level.

... and there may be scope for adjusting tax policies to help share costs and benefits more equitably...

4. CONCLUSIONS

This chapter has reviewed some of the key evidence for the relationship between human capital and economic and social outcomes. Inevitably, because of data constraints, the most robust measures of benefit and of returns focus on market outcomes only, and are based on formal educational attainment rather than on wider definitions of human capital investment. Notwithstanding the variety of complex inter-linking factors which underpin economic growth, the evidence does point to a positive relationship between expenditure for education and macroeconomic performance. But the mechanisms that create this impact, and hence the most effective types of investments in human capital, remain poorly understood. The most substantial finding is that tertiary education constitutes a relatively high cost to the taxpayer (per student), but appears to yield relatively high benefit to tertiary graduates.

Although the evidence is not clear-cut, it shows that there are positive benefits from human capital investment, which are not always proportionate to the distribution of costs.

The empirical evidence is weakest at two crucial points: 1) the wider social and economic benefits of education, and 2) the returns to individuals, organisations and societies for different types of learning in post-formal education settings. The following chapter looks further at these and other areas in which data need to be improved.

More needs to be known about the wider benefits and about returns to learning beyond schooling.

INDICATORS OF RETURNS TO INVESTMENT IN HUMAN CAPITAL

Indicator	What it shows	Usefulness and limitations	Data availability and sources	References in this volume
a) Employment-population ratio by level of educational attainment.	The proportion of employed in the total population of women aged 30-44 having attained particular levels of education.	One indicator of the labour market effects of more education. Particularly relevant for women. However, it focuses only on initial educational attainment.	Labour Force and Household Surveys.	Figure 4.1A and Table A4.1a in the Annex.
b) Unemployment expectancy by educational attainment.	Average expected number of years in unemployment for men over a working life by educational level attained.	Provides a crude indicator of the relative unemployment chances of different educational groups. However, estimates are based on current rates of unemployment across age-groups.	Labour Force and Household Surveys.	Figure 4.1B and Table A4.1b in the Annex.
c) Relative earnings by educational attainment.	Average annual earnings of 30-44 year olds with particular levels of educational attainment, relative to people with upper secondary education only. Men and women shown separately.	Shows wage premium associated with extra education for people in mid-career. However, it does not prove that this benefit is caused by the extra education or that it accurately reflects higher productivity.	Various Household Surveys relating income to educational attainment.	Figure 4.2 and Tables A4.2a and A4.2b in the Annex.
d) Correlation of literacy, education and labour market experience with earnings.	How much each of these factors contributes, independently of the others, to explaining differences in individual's earnings.	Makes it possible to compare the influence of educational background with directly measured skills and experience. However, relationships not well enough understood to draw very strong conclusions.	Data from the *International Adult Literacy Survey* for ten countries.	Table 4.1.
e) Impact of enterprise-based training.	Quantifiable effects of training on enterprise performance, earnings and job tenure.	Gives some indication, but not in a standardised form, of the extent to which firms and employees gain identifiable benefits from training.	Data from dispersed and non-standardised sources only.	Table 4.2.
f) Impact of public labour market programmes.	Quantifiable effects of such programmes on employment rates, pay, etc., of participants.	Gives some indication, but not in a standardised form, of the degree to which programmes achieve their objectives.	Evidence concentrated in North American based studies.	Table 4.3.
g) Annual rate of return to education.	Annual rate of return for completion of respective educational levels – based on public and private costs, and on the extra wages and associated tax revenues derived from the higher earnings of better educated groups.	Allows comparisons to be made of returns across countries and levels, and with returns to business capital. These however are indicative only because of various problems with measurement, and because wider social benefits (spill-over effects) are excluded.	Various Household Surveys relating income to educational attainment.	Figure 4.4 and Table A4.4.
h) "Fiscal" and "private" rates of return to education.	Rates of return that look respectively at only public and private costs and benefits.	Gives some preliminary indication of the relative returns to public and private interests. Further work is needed.	Preliminary data from various Household sources on income.	Discussion pp. 68-69.

NOTES

1. Differences in participation by women in employment are also explained by factors such as the availability of child care and other supports for working mothers.

2. Relatively higher rates of part-time employment among women with lower levels of educational attainment may also explain the relatively larger premium to highly-educated women.

3. Studies of identical twins such as that of Ashenfelter and Krueger (1994) have shown that the effects of controlling for ability, race, social class and family background are to lower estimated returns to education by about 25 per cent. However, other studies such as that by Ashenfelter and Rouse (forthcoming) show that error in the measurement of human capital acquired may lead to an under-estimation of rates of return by as much as 30 per cent (through for example omission of quality of education in the use of years of schooling as an explanatory variable). Therefore, measurement error and the omission of control variables in less sophisticated estimations of returns to education may tend to roughly cancel each other out.

4. Refer to p. 23 in Chapter 3 for description of literacy domains and scores.

5. Background factors such as age, gender and parental education were included as variables in the regression of earnings on literacy, educational attainment and work experience.

6. The findings of Hocquet (1997) that training followed by mobility leads to significantly higher wages seems to support the view that firms have little incentive to invest in general training. On other hand, Goux and Maurin (1997) found that firms which provide training are also those which pay higher wages, leading to lower probabilities of workers switching firms after training – thus providing evidence against the hypothesis that firms will not invest in general training.

7. Wagstaff (1986) shows similar results for Denmark.

8. The exceptionally low return to men for non-university tertiary education in the case of New Zealand is due to the higher level of earnings at upper secondary level compared to non-university level over some age-bands as well as a very low differential for other age-bands.

9. McMahon (1997) reports that total monetary and non-monetary annual rates of return in the mid-1990s amount to between 20-25 per cent at upper secondary education, and 26-28 per cent at university tertiary level in the United States. The value of the non-monetary return to education is based on what it would cost to produced the same outcome in other ways through, for example, purchasing health care (Wolfe and Zuvekas, 1997).

REFERENCES

ABT Associates (1993), *Longitudinal Study of Training Impacts for the Job Entry and Job Development Programs*, Program Evaluation Branch, Strategic Policy, Human Resources Development Canada, Hull, Canada, October.

ALSALAM, N. and CONLEY, R. (1995), "The rate of return to education: a proposal for an indicator", *Education and Employment*, Centre for Educational Research and Innovation, OECD, Paris.

ALTONJI, J. and PIERRET, C. (1996), "Employer learning and the signalling value of education", Working Paper No. 5438, National Bureau of Economic Research, Cambridge, Mass.

ASHENFELTER, O. and KREUGER, A. (1994), "Estimates of the economic return to schooling from a new sample of twins", *American Economic Review*, Vol. 84, pp. 1157-1173.

ASHENFELTER, O. and ROUSE, C. (forthcoming), "How convincing is the evidence linking education and income?", in O. Ashenfelter and C. Rouse (eds.), Cracks in the Bell Curve: Schooling, Intelligence, and Income.

BARNETT, S. (1995), "Long-term effects of early childhood programs on cognitive and school outcomes", *The Future of Children, Long-Term Outcomes of Early Childhood Programs*, Vol. 5, No. 3, Winter.

BARRETT, A. and O'CONNELL, P. (1997), "Does training generally work? Measuring the returns to in-company training", Working Paper No. 87, Economic and Social Research Institute, Dublin.

BARRO, R. and LEE, J. (1994), *Data Set for a Panel of 138 Countries*, Harvard University Press, Harvard.

BARRO, R. and SALA-I-MARTIN, X. (1995), *Economic Growth*, McGraw Hill, New York.

BARTEL, A. (1989), "Formal employee training programmes and their impact on labour productivity: Evidence from a human resources survey", Working Paper No. 3026, National Bureau of Economic Research, Cambridge, Mass.

BASSI, L. (1984), "Estimating the effects of training programs with non-random selection", *Review of Economics and Statistics*, Vol. 66, pp. 36-43.

BEHRMAN, J.R. and STACEY, N. (eds.) (1997), *The Social Benefits of Education*, The University of Michigan Press.

BETCHERMAN, G., LECKIE, N. and MCMULLEN, K. (1997), *Developing Skills in the Canadian Workplace: The Results of the Ekos Training Survey*, Canadian Policy Research Networks, Ottawa.

BETCHERMAN, G., McMULLEN, K., LECKIE, N. and CARON, C. (1994), *The Canadian Workplace in Transition*, Final Report of the Human Resource Management Project, Queens University Industrial Relations Centre, Kingston, Ontario.

BISHOP, J.H. (1994), "The impact of previous training on productivity and wage", in L.M. Lynch (ed.), *Training and the Private Sector: International Comparisons*, University of Chicago Press, Chicago, Illinois, pp. 185-186.

BISHOP, J.H. (1995), "The impact of curriculum-based external examinations on school priorities and student learning", Special issue of the *International Journal of Educational Research*.

BLACK, S. and LYNCH, L. (1996), "Human-capital investments and productivity", *American Economic Review*, Vol. 86, No. 2, pp. 263-267.

BLOOM, H.S. (1994), *The National JTPA Study: Overview of Impacts, Benefits and Costs of Title II-A.*, Abt Associates, Canada.

CALMFORS, L. (1994), "Active labour market policy and unemployment: A framework for the analysis of crucial design features", OECD *Economic Studies*, No. 22, Paris, Spring.

CARD, D. and SULLIVAN, D. (1988), "Measuring the effect of subsidised training programs on movements in and out of employment", *Econometrica*, Vol. 56, pp. 497-530.

CARR, C. (1992), "Productivity and skills in vehicle component manufacturers in Britain, Germany, the USA and Japan", *National Institute Economic Review*, February, pp. 79-87.

CHISWICK, B.R. (1991), "Speaking, reading and earnings among low skilled immigrants", Working Paper No. 5763, National Bureau of Economic Research, Cambridge, Mass.

DANISH MINISTRY OF BUSINESS AND INDUSTRY (1996), "Technological and organisational change – Implications for labour demand, enterprise performance and industrial policy", *The OECD Jobs Strategy*, Country Report, November, Copenhagen.

DECKER, P.T. and CORSON, W. (1995), "International trade and worker displacement: Evaluation of the trade adjustment assistance programme", *Industrial and Labour Relations Review*, Vol. 48, No. 4, July.

DENISON, E.F. (1962), *The Sources of Economic Growth in the United States and the Alternatives before Us*, Committee for Economic Development, New York.

DENISON, E.F. (1964), "Measuring the contribution of education", *The Residual Factor and Economic Growth*, OECD, Paris.

DESAI, S. (1987), "The estimation of the health production function for low-income working men", *Medical Care*, Vol. 25, pp. 604-615.

ENGLANDER, S. and GURNEY, A. (1994), "Medium-term determinants of OECD productivity", *OECD Economic Studies*, No. 22, OECD, Paris.

FAY, R.G. (1996), "Enhancing the effectiveness of active labour market policies: Evidence from programme evaluations in OECD countries", Labour Market and Social Policy Occasional Papers, No. 18, OECD, Paris.

FELDMAN, J., MAKUC, D., KLEINMAN, J. and CORNONI-HUXLEY, J. (1989), "National trends in educational differentials in mortality", *American Journal of Epidemiology*, Vol. 129, pp. 919-933.

FREEMAN, R. and KATZ, L. (eds.) (1995), *Differences and Changes in Wage Structures*, University of Chicago Press, Chicago.

GOTTSCHALK, P. and JOYCE, M. (1997), "Crossnational differences in the rise in earnings inequality – Market and institutional factors", LIS Working Paper No. 160, Luxembourg Income Study, Luxembourg.

GOUX, G. and MAURIN, E. (1997), "Train or pay: Does it reduce inequalities to encourage firms to train their workers?", Paper presented to the CEPR Workshop "Rising Inequalities", La Coruna, 14-15 February.

GROOT, W. (1994), "Bedrijfsopleidingen goed vorr loon and productiviteit", *Economisch Statistische Berichten*, No. 3988, pp. 1108-1111.

GROOT, W. and HARTOG, J. (1995), "Screening models and education", in Carnoy, M. (ed.), *International Encyclopedia of Economics of Education*, Pergamon Press, Oxford.

GROOT, W. and OOSTERBEEK, H. (1995), "Determinants and wages effects of different components of participation in on- and off-the-job training", Research Memorandum, Tinbergen Institute, Rotterdam, pp. 95-112.

GROSSMAN, M. (1975), "The correlation between health and schooling", in N.E. Terleckyj (ed.), *Household Production and Consumption*, Studies in Income and Wealth, University Press for the National Bureau of Economic Research, pp. 147-211.

GROSSMAN, M. and KAESTNER, R. (1996), "Effects of Education on Health", in Behrman, J.R. and Stacey, N. (eds.), *The Social Benefits of Education*, University of Pennsylvania, Philadelphia.

HOCQUET, L. (1997), "Vocational training and the poaching externality: Evidence for France", Paper presented to the CEPR Workshop "Rising Inequalities", La Coruna, 14-15 February.

HOLZER, H., BLOCK, R., CHEATHAM, M. and KNOTT, J. (1993), "Are training subsidies for firms effective? The Michigan experience", *Industrial and Labour Relations Review*, Vol. 46.

HUMAN RESOURCES DEVELOPMENT CANADA (1995), *Evaluation of the Employability Improvement Programme*, Hull, Canada.

HUMAN RESOURCES DEVELOPMENT CANADA and OECD (1996), *Changing Workplace Strategies: Achieving Better Outcomes for Enterprises, Workers and Society*, Hull, Canada, December.

ICHNIOWSKI, C., SHAW, K. and PRENNUSHI, G. (1994), "The effects of human resource management practices on productivity", Working Paper, Columbia University, New York.

JACOBSON, L.S., LALONDE, R.J., SULLIVAN, D.G. and BEDNARZIK, R. (1994), "The returns from classroom training for displaced workers", mimeo.

JACOBSON, R. (1995), "What can active labour market policy do?", Centre for Economic Performance, Discussion Paper No. 226.

JENSEN, P., PEDERSEN, P., SMITH, N. and WESTERGARD-NIELSEN, N. (1990), "Measuring the effects of labour market training programmes", mimeo, Department of Economics, University of Aarhus.

JORGENSON, D. W. and GRILICHES, Z. (1967), "The explanation of productivity change", *Review of Economic Studies*, Vol. 34, pp. 249-280, July.

KLING, J. (1995), "High performance work systems and firm performance", *Monthly Labour Review*, U.S. Department of Labour, May.

LALONDE, R.J. (1995), "The promise of public sector-sponsored training programs", *The Journal of Economic Perspectives*, Vol. 9 (2), pp. 149-169.

LAU, L., JAMISON, D. and LOUAT, F. (1991), "Education and productivity in developing countries: an aggregate production function approach", Working Paper No. 612, World Bank, Washington, DC.

 LAULHÉ, P. (1990), "La formation continue : un avantage pour les promotions à un accès privilégié pour les jeunes et les techniciens", *Économie et Statistiques*, pp. 3-8.

LIEBFRITZ, W., THORNTON, J. and BIBBEE, A. (1997), "Taxation and economic performance", Economics Department Working Papers, No. 176, OECD, Paris.

LOEWENTSTEIN, M. and SPLETZER, J. (1997), "General and specific training: Evidence and implications", mimeo, Bureau of Labour Statistics, Washington, DC.

LUCAS, R.E. (1988), "On the mechanics of economic development", *Journal of Monetary Economics*, Vol. 22, pp. 3-42.

LUND, R. and GJERDING, A. (1996), "The flexible company: Innovation, work organisation, and human resource management", Prepared for the international conference on Changing Workplace Strategies.

MANKIW, N., ROMER, D. and WEIL, D. (1992), "A contribution to the empirics of economic growth", *Quarterly Journal of Economics*, Vol. CVII, pp. 407-437.

MASON, G., VAN ARK, B. and WAGNER, K. (1994), "Productivity, product quality and workforce skills: Food processing in four European countries", *National Institute Economic Review*, February, pp. 62-96.

MILLER, P.W. and PINCUS, J.J. (1998), "Super HECS: A proposal for funding Australian higher education", in P.W. Miller and J.J. Pincus (eds.), *Financing Higher Education – Performance and Diversity*, DEETYA (forthcoming).

MINCER, J. (1996), "Changes in wage inequality, 1970-1990", Working Paper 5823, National Bureau of Economic Research, Cambridge, Mass.

MINGAT, A. and TAN, J. (1996), "The full social returns to education: Estimates based on countries' economic growth performance", *Human Capital Development Working Papers*, World Bank, Washington, DC.

Mc MAHON, W. (1991) "Relative returns to human and physical capital in the US and efficient investment strategies", *Economics of Education Review*, Vol. 10, No. 4, pp. 283-296.

Mc MAHON, W. (1997) "Recent advances in measuring the social and individual benefits of education", *International Journal of Educational Research*, Vol. 27, No. 6, Chapter 1.

NATIONAL BUREAU of ECONOMIC RESEARCH (1996), "Small research groups: growth", National Bureau of Economic Research Reporter, Cambridge, Mass., Fall.

NATIONAL CENTER for HEALTH STATISTICS (1996), *Vital and Health Statistics*, Series 10, No. 195, Center for Disease Control and Prevention, US Department of Health and Human Services.

NEHRU, V., SWANSON, E. and DUBEY, A. (1993), A *New Database on Human Capital Stock, Sources, Methodology and Results*, Policy Research Working Paper, International Economics Department, World Bank, Washington, DC.

NONNEMAN, W. and VANHOUDT, P. (1996), "A further augmentation of the Solow model and the empirics of economic growth for OECD countries", *Quarterly Journal of Economics*, pp. 943-953.

OECD (1993), *Employment Outlook*, Paris.

OECD (1994), *The OECD Jobs Study, Evidence and Explanations, Part II*, Paris

OECD (1997a), *Education at a Glance – OECD Indicators*, Paris.

OECD (1997b), *Education Policy Analysis*, Paris

OECD (1997c), *Economic Outlook*, Paris.

OECD, Human Resource Development Canada and Statistics Canada (1997), *Literacy Skills for a Knowledge Society – Further Results from the International Adult Literacy Survey*, Paris.

O'CONNELL, P. and McGINNITY, F. (1997), *Working Schemes? Active Labour Market Policy in Ireland*, Ashgate, Aldershot.

O'MAHONEY, M. (1992), "Productivity levels in British and German manufacturing industry", *National Institute Economic Review*, February.

OTTERSTEN KAZAMAKI, E., LINDH, T. and MELLANDER E. (1996), "Cost and productivity effects of firm financed training", Industrial Institute for Economic and Social Research Working Paper No. 455, Uppsala, Sweden.

PAYNE, J., LISSENBURGH, S., WHITE, M. and PAYNE, C. (1996), "Employment training and employment action: An evaluation by matched comparison method", Department for Education and Employment, Research Series No. 74, Sheffield.

PSACHAROPOULOS, G. (1994), "Returns to investment in education: a global update", *World Development*, Vol. 22 (9), pp. 1325-1343, September.

RAAUM, O., TORP, H. and GOLDSTEIN, H. (1995), "Effects of labour market training: A multinomial analysis", Working Paper No. 9/95, University of Oslo.

ROSENZWEIG, M.R. and SCHULTZ, T.P. (1991), "Who receives medical care? Income, implicit prices, and the distribution of medical services among pregnant women in the United States", *Journal of Human Resources*, Vol. 26, pp. 473-508.

RUSSELL, J., TERBORG, J. and POWERS, M. (1985), "Organizational performance and organizational level training and support", *Personnel Psychology*.

RYAN, P. and BUECHTMANN, C. (1996), "The school to work transition", in G. Schmid, J. O'Reilly and K. Schoemann (eds.), *International Handbook of Labour Market Policy and Evaluation*, Edward Elgar, Cheltenahm, pp. 308-347.

SCARPETTA, S. (1996), "Assessing the role of labour market policies and settings on unemployment: a cross-country study", OECD *Economic Studies*, No. 26, OECD, Paris.

SPENCE, M. (1974), *Market Signaling*, Harvard University Press, Cambridge, Mass.

TANÁS, A., HARKMAN, A. and JANNSON, F. (1995), "The effect of vocationally oriented employment training on income and employment", Arbetsmarknadsstyrelsen.

TAUBMAN, P. and ROSEN, S. (1982), "Healthiness, education and marital status", in V.R. Fuchs (ed.), *Economic Aspects of Health*, University of Chicago Press for the NBER, Chicago, pp. 121-140.

WAGSTAFF, A. (1986), "The demand for health: Some new empirical evidence", *Journal of Health Economics*, Vol. 5, pp. 195-233.

WOLFE, B. and ZUVEKAS, S. (1997), "Non-market outcomes of schooling", *International Journal of Educational Research*, Vol. 27, No. 6, Chapter 3.

ZILL, N. (1994), "Characteristics of teenage mothers", Talking Points for the American Enterprise Institute Conference on the Costs of Teenage Child Bearings.

IMPROVING THE KNOWLEDGE BASE: INDICATORS, DATA AND RESEARCH NEEDS

1. IDENTIFYING THE PRINCIPAL GAPS

Human capital as defined in this report can never be measured precisely. However, there is considerable scope for building on what is known about human capital stocks, investments and returns. Of particular interest to policy are indicators of where the most serious shortfalls in stocks occur, and of the relationship between the cost of investing in these areas and the resulting benefits.

There is scope to build on existing knowledge...

Internationally comparable data on the operation of education and training systems have been greatly strengthened in recent years, led by the OECD programme on international indicators of education systems (INES). These indicators now give good information on the quantity and cost of investment in formal education, and although measurement of these quantities over time have so far been weak, they are improving. Knowledge about less formal learning, including that which takes place at work, has of its nature been harder to quantify and aggregate. Moreover, direct measures of people's knowledge, skills and competencies have been relatively weak at an international level, although they are being improved. Estimates of returns are still at a highly developmental stage, and do not yet take account of the full range of social benefits.

... which has been strengthened for formal education but elsewhere remains weak.

To achieve a better understanding and measurement of human capital, it is necessary to develop direct measures of skill, competence and aptitudes, as well as the broad social and economic impact of human capital. It is insufficient to measure only the amount of education undertaken, or the number of people who obtain educational qualifications. Such qualifications certify, in the different context of each country's education system, acquisition of certain types of knowledge and skill, but do not systematically measure a broader range of economically-relevant skills

In improving knowledge on human capital, a two-pronged strategy is called for. First, there needs to be a continuation of existing efforts to improve incrementally the quality and scope of education indicators. Although this is

Priority should be given first to developing more direct measures of relevant skills...

partly a matter of refining existing measures and improving their comparability, priority should be given to developing new measures of skills, competencies and aptitudes, and better indicators of relationships between these attributes and labour market experiences particularly in the context of lifelong learning for all.

... and second to looking in more detail at how acquiring human capital brings labour market benefits.

It will always be difficult to get a full understanding of such relationships through aggregate indicators alone. A second part of the strategy therefore needs to consist of more targeted research bringing together comparable information from a range of countries. Such research may look for example at particular enterprises or sectors to examine the contribution of various types of competence to productivity. While such an approach will be appropriate for case-study research, the results would be useful in highlighting important gaps in existing knowledge about outcomes.

Such methods need to be used to extend knowledge about human capital investment in two ways in particular: first to improve understanding of the outcomes of learning in terms of individual attributes; second, to obtain better estimates of economic benefits and returns.

2. FROM MEASURING PARTICIPATION IN EDUCATION AND TRAINING TO MEASURING HUMAN CAPITAL

Using formal education as a proxy for human capital formation begs the issue of the quality and relevance of education systems...

Estimates of both the stock and the rate of formation of human capital have most frequently used years of schooling or completion of an educational level as the best available proxy. Measures of adult education and training activity can also implicitly equate the taking part in such activity with the formation of human capital. However, participation in formal learning is only a good proxy for the acquisition of economically-relevant knowledge, skills, competencies and aptitudes if all learning is similar in quality and objectives. Making this assumption begs the question of how the quality and pertinence of nations' learning systems can be improved. It also ignores the importance of learning outside formal education and training.

... and educational qualifications mean different things in different countries, do not certify economic value and ignore depreciation...

Measures of educational attainment in principle go further towards expressing educational outcomes than years spent studying. A certificate of upper secondary education, for example, registers the fact that a student has passed certain courses and exams, not just that he or she has spent a certain amount of time studying. As a proxy measure of human capital, however, attainment is also insufficient, for at least three reasons:

a) when comparing attainment across countries, there is no consistent definition of what a particular level means in terms of knowledge and skills;

b) the knowledge and skills represented by attainment are defined by education systems with, at most, indirect reference to which attributes will have economic value;

c) a person's qualifications are kept for life, but the qualities required to gain them may depreciate over time.

As a result, there is a strong case for improving the direct measurement of the attributes in individuals that compose human capital. These measures can be used to produce indicators of educational outcomes, but that is not their only purpose. When applied to the adult population, they measure attributes acquired through a range of experiences not just in formal education but also in family, community and work settings. By also collecting background information about participants in such surveys, it is possible to discern the relative importance of these different influences on various aspects of human capital.

... so, direct measures of people's attributes are needed...

Three approaches are at present being developed, based around international surveys that test:

– *Student achievement in particular areas of knowledge and competence at different stages of school education.* Chapter 2 referred to achievement data in mathematics and science for 9 and 13 year olds, and the data will be extended in the future to include 15 year olds. This kind of test is attractive to governments because it addresses the first of the problems with attainment measures referred to above: it gives a common yardstick against which to judge education systems' performance in meeting some of their basic objectives. However, such tests on their own give only a partial picture of attributes relevant to economic activity, and take no account of depreciation of skills during adulthood.

... and tests are now being developed – for schoolchildren both in school subjects and in wider skills, and for adults in various relevant competences.

– *Competences of school-age children that cross the boundaries defined by subject curricula.* The OECD has already laid the basis for new measurement and data collection through planned indicators on "cross-curricular competences" such as problem-solving, communication, teamwork, knowledge of democratic and economic systems, and self-esteem. This ambitious project aims to give a more complete picture of the human capital conferred by school systems in different countries – and thus to address both points *a*) and *b*) above, although not point *c*). Given the stage of current developments, it will be well into the next decade before the first results are available, and longer still before robust comparative findings can be generated.

– *Adult skills and competences relevant to everyday life and work.* The *International Adult Literacy Survey* (IALS), for which results have so far been published for 12 countries, has made it possible to compare skills in a number of domains (see Chapter 2 above). Further work remains to be done in extending the range of measures to include inter-personal skills, problem-solving and other aptitudes not covered by the various types of literacy skills measured by IALS. This work is progressing through the *International Life Skills Survey* which is being tested in the near future with a view to further development thereafter. Such surveys address all of points *a*) to *c*) above, and by collecting background information on participants, they are capable of showing associations between demonstrated features of human capital and the types of learning programmes in which individuals have participated. However, since they are not carried out immediately after completion of these programmes, they offer only an approximation of their impact on skills, and cannot fully monitor the effectiveness of basic education.

These tests are not cheap, but can provide value for money.

Collecting information in all three of these categories implies an extension of present work on indicators through the development of new surveys. Although there are significant resource implications, value for money can potentially be maximised by adapting the same test instruments to serve as policy tools within a national context and to yield international comparisons. The issue of costs is discussed further in section 3 below.

3. COMPARING INVESTMENT COSTS WITH BENEFITS

It is important, if difficult, to compare returns to different forms of learning.

While there is clear evidence that investment in human capital yields benefits, it remains difficult to calculate precise rates of return from particular investments. The central problem lies in attributing specific economic gains to particular human attributes, and link these in confidence with particular learning episodes. It is nevertheless desirable to develop at least some measures that can compare alternative human capital investments in terms of their respective costs and benefits. Otherwise, there is the risk of assuming that because investment in learning as a whole seems to pay off, it is equally worthwhile in all its forms.

The illustrative rates of return presented in Chapter 4 are of value in showing that significant net benefits can accrue from investments in education, but that the return on the costs borne publicly and privately can be highly variable. The main difficulty in looking at rates of return at present is that they can only be constructed with the easiest-to-aggregate data. They leave out the full range of social benefits, and only apply to differences in educational attainment, wholly ignoring aspects of human capital that are not linked to initial qualifications.

While quantifiable rates of return are likely to remain crude and incomplete, approximations for some time to come, there is considerable value in seeking better data to fill out a highly incomplete picture of the costs and benefits associated with various types of learning. One priority is to obtain better aggregate information about how much is being invested by individuals and enterprises in various forms of learning. Another is to improve understanding of the individual and wider economic benefits associated with learning in work-based and other non-institutional settings. Longitudinal data tracing the experience of individuals over different points in time would be valuable in measuring the extent to which different skills are acquired or lost as they are used or not used in different occupations and settings. This type of information is most amenable to qualitative research, some of which is already being undertaken, but which could be co-ordinated more systematically in an international framework.

Table 5.1 shows the uneven state of existing knowledge which is strongest for formal education...

Table 5.1 summarises the state of existing knowledge on the costs and benefits associated with different kinds of human capital investment. It shows that there is at present good knowledge of the investments made by governments, but much less about costs borne by individuals and enterprises, which are important in the case of post-compulsory formal education, and dominant in the case of work-based and informal learning. On the benefits side, there is good information on individual gains from initial education and from labour market training programmes, but not from other forms of work-related training. The broader social and economic benefits have not been well quantified for any kind of human capital investment.

Looking first at *initial education* from early childhood through to higher education, there is relatively abundant information on public investments and the aggregate effect on job and pay prospects. However, more information is needed in particular on:

... although data is still patchy on social benefits, on private investment levels and on different returns to various forms of study.

–   *Social benefits.* As described in Chapter 4, a number of studies have demonstrated that it is possible to identify benefits of human capital investment in terms, for example, of better levels of health. However, these studies have been mainly limited to North America, and there is considerable potential for improving the knowledge base internationally.

–   *Levels of private investment.* Contributions from individuals, families and firms to the cost of education are not as well quantified as the public cost. In the case of post-compulsory education, this includes forgone earnings. Tuition fee payments by households at post-compulsory level education are better measured.

–   *Information on outcomes from different types of upper-secondary and tertiary level programme.* To obtain a better understanding of pathways taken through education, training and the labour market, more detailed historical information is needed, through household surveys or longitudinal surveys tracking individuals from education to their early years in the labour market. Although the latter option is costly, and longitudinal surveys would have to be organised at an international level to obtain comparable information across countries, they constitute a potentially rich source of information on diverse matters of policy interest. However, underlying changes in labour market conditions may limit the usefulness or relevance of results based on longitudinal studies from which results cannot be obtained except over a long period of time.

In *public labour market training programmes* and other active labour market policies, the main direct and indirect costs are typically borne by public authorities through identifiable budgets. The substantial time investments made by individuals are hard to value, since it is difficult to determine whether participants would otherwise have been in a position to earn. Of greater interest is the impact of such programmes in terms of improving pay and employment prospects for various types of participant, about which evidence is growing. However, many countries still do not rigorously evaluate programmes, with respect to their effectiveness and efficiency. Moreover, comparative international research could help to expand knowledge of what works, and ensure that effectiveness is well scrutinised.

For public training programmes, the direct costs are better documented than indirect ones or benefits...

Investments in enterprise-related training are widely dispersed among individuals, firms and governments. There is limited evidence on the scale of expenditure by different actors. Evidence on benefits is also limited, although there is a growing body of survey data on increases in wages to individuals and productivity gains for employers (see Chapter 4 above). Information on both investments and benefits is at present limited to a small number of countries, and there is scope for extending research internationally. The joint work between the Australian Bureau of Statistics and OECD which led to the *Manual for Better Training Statistics* (OECD, 1997a), needs to be followed up by the development of a multi-purpose module on training for use in different types of international and national surveys.

... for enterprise-based training, information on both investment and benefits needs improving...

Table 5.1. **A framework for assessing costs and benefits of human capital investment**

	Individuals		Enterprises		Government/society	
	Costs	Benefits	Costs	Benefits	Costs	Benefits
Early childhood education	Fees, forgone earnings of parents	Foundation skills	–	–	Direct outlays on nursery schools	Foundation for learning and social cohesion
Data availability	Limited	Some research findings	–	–	Public finance accounts	Limited
Compulsory education	Tuition fees and other educational costs	Future productive and social capabilities and better quality of life	Some direct financial contributions	Improved skills, cognitive and behavioural attribues of workers	Direct outlays	Higher skill levels, social cohesion, economic growth and tax returns
Data availability	Limited information based on household surveys	Household survey data on labour market performance and earnings of individuals	Generally not available	Limited data from enterprise surveys on impact on performance	Public finance accounts	Estimates of additional taxes based on income survey data (but little on economic and social spin-offs)
Post-compulsory and higher education	Tuition fees, other educational costs and forgone earnings while in study	Skills/qualifications leading to higher earnings, employability and quality of life	Direct financial contributions	Improved skills, cognitive and behafviour attributes of workers	Direct outlays on educational institutions, transfers to students	Higher skill levels, social cohesion, economic growth and tax returns
Data availability	Very limited information based on household surveys	Survey data on labour market performance and earnings of individuals	Generally not available	Limited data from enterprise surveys on impact on performance	Public finance accounts	Estimates of additional taxes based on income survey data (but little on economic and social spin-offs)
Public labour market training programmes	Tuition fees, other training costs and forgone earnings	Skills/qualifications leading to higher earnings	Some direct financial contributions	Improved cognitive and behavioural attributes of workers	Direct outlays	Higher skill level, social cohesion, economic growth and tax returns
Data availability	Limited information	Growing empirical literature on effects on employment and earnings	Not available	Limited information	Public finance account	Limited information
Research and development	No cost	Skill enhancements, some earnings increases, mobility potential	Direct outlays	Enhanced performance and competitiveness	Direct outlays	Enhanced competitiveness, development of the knowledge base
Data availability	–	–	Direct financial contributions to R&D	Limited data from patent surveys, innovation surveys	Public finance accounts	Limited research findings

Table 5.1. **A framework for assessing costs and benefits of human capital investment** (*continued*)

	Individuals		Enterprises		Government/society	
	Costs	*Benefits*	*Costs*	*Benefits*	*Costs*	*Benefits*
Enterprise training	Zero to full cost, depending on terms of contract	Studies suggest positive impact on wages, job tenure and productivity	Direct outlays, wages paid and some training levies	Enterprise-specific knowledge with improvements in productivity	Zero to full subsidy	Higher skill levels, social cohesion, economic growth and tax returns
Data availability	Limited information (household surveys)	Limited information (household surveys)	Limited information (administrative or enterprise surveys)	Limited information (enterprise surveys)	Public finance accounts	Little information
Informal learning	Opportunity time costs and direct financial costs	Economic and non-economic gains depending on qualifications earned	Cost of lost production time due to learning	Enterprise-specific knowledge with improvements in productivity	No cost	Economic and social spin-offs
Data availability	Limited availability from household surveys	Limited availability	Limited availability	Enterprise-specific knowledge with improvements in productivity	–	Little information

The impact of human capital in enterprises could be analysed through the development of more interactive data sets linking administrative, employee and workplace data as well as the development of more cross-country comparisons of enterprises, controlling for underlying characteristics of firms. This could be extended through comprehensive international surveys, or through the linking of narrow-purpose surveys to focus on relationships between skills, training and characteristics of workers and firms. Although these would take time to develop, and could well be relatively costly, once established they could provide a very rich source of information.

... and by developing new ways of presenting human capital investment and assets in public and private accounts...

Better information could be useful for making not just public but also private choices. Lack of information hinders rational and effective human capital investment strategies; this is particularly true of enterprises. Knowledge, whether embodied in the workforce or at the level of the firm, accounts for an increasing share of total company asset value – yet this is poorly measured. If human capital were to be more explicitly reflected in national, corporate and public accounting systems, enterprises would be able to report externally, to capital markets in particular, on the extent and use of intangible assets. Non-mandatory reporting by enterprises of human capital should therefore be examined. At government level, the treatment in national and other public accounts of outlays for education and training mainly as consumption, rather than as investment in a vital asset contributing to future national income, needs to be reviewed.

... and lastly, new OECD work is starting to clarify the contribution of R&D.

Finally, despite some progress, there remains a lack of empirical evidence dealing with investment in enterprise-based research and development. It is difficult to measure all R&D, which is not always sufficiently discrete to be separated out from other economic activity. It is also difficult to assess the knowledge embodied in firms and research organisations, as well as in networks that contribute to a whole that is greater than the individuals constituting them. These difficulties notwithstanding, there is promising new OECD work involving international comparisons of knowledge flows in national innovation systems, new science and technology indicators for the knowledge-based economy, and sectoral case studies focusing on knowledge production, mediation and use (OECD 1997b,c).

4. THE COST OF DATA COLLECTION

The potentially high cost of adequate indicators could be contained by:

An underlying issue of concern to ministers is the cost of extra data collection. At its most ambitious, a comprehensive strategy for measuring every aspect of human capital could cost millions if not billions of dollars. In practice, the cost can be contained to much more modest proportions in several ways:

... concentrating on measuring those competences shown to be most important...

–   *First by focusing surveys on areas of greatest priority.* In particular, they need to concentrate on measuring quantitatively those elements of human capital found through qualitative research at different levels (*e.g.* enterprises, industry sectors and individuals) to be the most important in raising employment and productivity. For example, the planned OECD survey of life skills is being designed around those competences, such as problem-solving abilities that are shown by workplace studies to be most beneficial.

- *Second, by aiming to improve the integration between national and international data and research exercises.* Some integration has already been achieved in the collection of information on labour markets through Labour Force Surveys. The co-ordination by the OECD of nationally-based surveys of adult literacy, life skills and student achievement are showing how such principles can be extended to large testing exercises. In general, there is a move from submitting nationally defined data to respond to international requests, towards co-operation across countries on the definition and design of indicators. Since there is not an exact correspondence between questions of interest at national and international levels, international collaboration is not cost-free, but an integrated approach can greatly reduce the additional costs.

… co-ordinating existing and new research and data collection across countries…

- *Third, by rationalising existing data collection within and among countries.* There is considerable scope, for example, for co-ordinating diverse surveys on enterprise training. It is also possible to co-ordinate several national research programmes with common objectives, to give comparators in other countries. So, even in the case of qualitative research based around case studies, there is considerable scope for obtaining more comparable findings across countries, providing the research is set up in a common framework.

… and avoiding duplication while improving comparability.

5. CONCLUSION: BALANCING MEASUREMENT AND UNDERSTANDING

Measures of human capital have been strongly guided by what is possible to measure, rather than by what it is desirable to measure. As a result, much analysis has focused on the benefits of initial educational attainment to individuals, rather than on the more complex relationships between lifetime development of skills and competencies on the one hand, and the multiple advantages conferred by these attributes on the other. The priority now should be to develop more direct measures of life-relevant skills, of the value placed on them in the workplace and of the benefits to individuals and enterprises of work-related training.

There needs to be a focus on the most significant rather than just the most measurable features of human capital…

The two-pronged strategy suggested in this chapter is based on twin changes to the traditional measurement model. First, the technical capacity is being developed to create broader measures of stocks and investments. In particular, new surveys are being pioneered that directly measure complex features of human capital stocks rather than relying on educational attainment as a proxy. One dimension, literacy, has already been reported on, and the ability to measure more complex aspects of life skills is being developed. New aggregate indicators based on surveys could also give a more complete picture of investment, bringing together more information on the cost to private individuals and enterprises. Second, however, it should be accepted that a full understanding of the relationships between investments and benefits cannot be obtained purely by aggregate data. More micro-level analysis, combining qualitative case studies with quantitative surveys needs to explore in particular the benefits to individuals, firms and societies that arise from human capital formation, and where possible to link these benefits more precisely to skills gained from particular learning programmes. With the help of this more detailed understanding, knowledge about human capital will be even more important to policy makers, companies and individuals in taking investment decisions.

… both by taking advantage of new direct measurement techniques and by examining in more detail the complex processes that give value to human capital.

REFERENCES

OECD (1997a), *Manual for Better Training Statistics – Conceptual, Measurement and Survey Issues*, Paris.

OECD (1997b), "National innovations systems", free document, Directorate for Science, Technology and Industry.

OECD (1997c), "Progress report on the 'New S&T indicators for the knowledge-based economy' activity", document for the NESTI Group meeting, Directorate for Science, Technology and Industry, June.

HUMAN CAPITAL INVESTMENT: POLICY ISSUES AND QUESTIONS

1. THE POLICY CONTEXT

OECD societies are transforming in ways that make human attributes central to economic prosperity. The competence of a nation's workers is coming to be at least as important to its success as other advantages such as the availability of land and capital. For growth and prosperity to be sustainable, social cohesion is required; here too, the role of human capital is vital. These tenets are now increasingly accepted. However, understanding of the precise economic and social contribution made by various kinds of human capital investment is highly imperfect.

There is growing recognition of the key role of human capital in economic growth and social cohesion.

It is in the interest of governments to improve this understanding. Their strategies for promoting learning across populations should draw on a new model of the relationships between human competence and economic success appropriate to the "knowledge economy". As rapid change causes current knowledge and competence to depreciate faster, the objective of "lifelong learning" has been adopted in order to ensure that human capital is regularly renewed. Yet, the development of measures of human capital lags behind this change. The level of education attained in youth remains a more convenient measure than a calculation of how skills and competences are gained and lost throughout life. The logic of a broad definition of human capital is that no single measure can serve. A complex set of relationships, determining not only the accumulation but also the use of skills and other attributes, need to be understood.

Governments can influence the development of human capital in many ways even though their influence is one of many, and must be exercised in partnership with other interested parties. In considering strategically which forms of learning most need support or encouragement, governments should be able to judge the relative desirability of different activities in terms of their public and private costs and their public and private benefits.

Governments have a key role in guiding investment choices.

The evidence currently available, which is reviewed in earlier chapters, does not produce clear-cut policy messages. However, a number of points emerge which should inform policy thinking about human capital investment. In particular, it is clear that:

Human capital investment accounts for a significant part of total national income.

– A *substantial proportion of national income is devoted to investment in human capital.* Public and private spending on formal education and training are on average about 6 per cent of GDP. Companies allocate about 2 per cent of their paybill to training their workers. However as well as this readily identifiable spending, considerable resources in terms of the time of families and individuals are devoted to the improvement of knowledge, skills and competence. So, the stakes are high: it is critical to ensure that this volume of effort is well-directed.

There is considerable private investment in human capital though it is not fully accounted for.

– *Investment in human capital is a shared enterprise.* Although most of the reported spending on formal education remains public, private investments are taking a more equal part in post-compulsory education and training, and are dominant in the case of enterprise-based training. Since public and private interests overlap, and learning undertaken for one purpose can have spin-off effects for others, this points to the need for partnership.

There are significant social and economic returns to investment…

– *Overall, returns can be substantial.* The data on rates of return to education illustrate how high public and private outlays can be rewarded by high gains, at least in the case of the relative earnings of employed individuals with different levels of initial education. On the whole, the estimated rates of return compare favourably with returns to other investments, implying that even in pure economic terms, investment in learning is worthwhile. Even higher returns may be identified if social benefits were taken into account, or if the measures specifically reflected activities directly aimed at improving job skills rather than general educational attainment.

… however, human capital is not equitably distributed within countries.

– *The distribution of human capital is worryingly skewed.* Looked at in terms of scholastic achievement, by the age of 13, the lowest-achieving quarter of young people are behind the highest-achieving quarter by the equivalent of three to four years of schooling, even within individual countries. Across countries the gap is even greater. Looked at in terms of the skills of adults, typically between one third and one half lack the kinds of literacy skills that are needed to function well in modern societies. By no means do all those in this latter group have low levels of education, implying that raising educational attainment will not on its own produce adequate levels of human capital.

2. FIVE POLICY ISSUES

Such findings raise a number of challenges for governments which should consider the following points: levels of human capital investment; the nature of, and scope for co-investment; optimising the public outlays; and ensuring more equitable outcomes.

i) Adequate levels of human capital investment

It is difficult to calculate what level of human capital investment best meets an economy's needs. However, governments are bound to make judgements about whether enough attention is being devoted to certain strategically important areas of learning activity, as well as considering whether the skill level of the population is sufficient. The indicators presented in this report start to create benchmarks, although better ones are needed. Two key shortfalls should concern any country. First, the numbers of adults who have not attained upper-secondary education and are therefore likely to lack the foundation needed to build up their human capital. Second, the proportion of the population who do not display the level of literacy and other skills needed to tackle the demands of 21st century life and work. The first measure indicates adults' capacity for extending, the second their capacity for using human capital. The biggest missing pieces in the jigsaw puzzle are measures of opportunities to extend human capital at work, and of the benefits that result from work-based learning. There are strong indications of positive economic results for individuals and firms, but better knowledge would help create more and better-directed investment.

It is difficult to establish benchmarks.

In situations where there appears to be under-investment in human capital – in a country as a whole, in particular localities or key sectors of the economy – there is a range of options that governments might take other than directly providing courses. Options to be explored include, *e.g.* re-examining taxation systems in order to give further incentives to individuals and enterprises to invest in human capital. The incentives for enterprises and workers to invest in human capital could also be improved by enabling workers "to alternate between work and extended periods of off-the-job training over their working life – *e.g.* through reductions in working time that are compensated by increases in training time" (OECD *Job Study: Facts, Analysis, and Strategies*, 1994, page 48).

A range of policy options are available to encourage investment in human capital.

ii) Appropriate sharing of investment costs

No single sector has a monopoly on human capital investment. The investments made by individuals, families, enterprises and public authorities all contribute to the total stock of human capital. Investment by governments is most appropriate where public benefits are likely to be high, while individuals and enterprises need to take significant responsibility for learning with high private returns. However, different learning experiences are mutually reinforcing, and many bring a combination of public and private gains. Partnerships are needed that match shared interests with shared investments. Calculations of public and private rates of return can help clarify whether existing patterns of cost-sharing are appropriate. In areas such as tertiary education for young people where investments are primarily public but large private gains accrue, it is legitimate to ask whether cost-sharing should be adjusted. In doing so, however, due account should be taken of aspects of existing private costs (such as forgone earnings) and public benefits (such as spin-off social gains) that are not always fully reported. Conversely, for investments such as enterprise-based training that are currently financed primarily by the private sector, public gains from increased tax revenues or spin-off effects arising from economic growth need to be recognised. Better measurement of these benefits will help governments evaluate the case for public support for such training where markets alone fail to optimise investment.

Better measurement of returns could inform decisions about the most appropriate sharing of costs and responsibilities.

In cases where cost-sharing creates the need for active partnerships, many issues arise other than financial ones. Governments need to review their strategies in building up the effectiveness of partnership ventures, and consider how they can play supportive roles when they are not the lead partner.

iii) Optimal allocation of scarce resources in relation to the costs and benefits of alternative investments

Returns are unequal across levels of initial education and different learning environments.

Evidence on rates of return shows that a dollar of investment will not always produce the same amount of human capital, however measured. Existing indicators are far from perfect, but they nevertheless provoke salient questions. For example, the high individual gains associated with participation in tertiary education, when set against their high costs and forgone earnings, do not necessarily yield the highest returns. Initial calculations indicate that individual and "social" rates of return are frequently inferior to those associated with completing upper secondary education (such calculations are, however, based only on readily-quantified variables). Neither is it clear why some countries spend over three times as much per student in tertiary education than in primary education, whereas others spend about the same. The rationale for such patterns needs to be made clearer, and linked to analysis of benefits.

"Market failure" may lead to under-investment by companies in work-based training.

It is also important to look carefully at both the costs and benefits of supporting various forms of work-related training. There is by no means clear evidence that active labour market programmes always provide good value overall, although there is greater evidence of benefits for individuals than there is evidence of social benefits. In considering wider support for enterprise-based training, policies should consider what is best left to the market and where there is "market failure" in the form of under-investment. The latter may occur, for example, because firms are unwilling to train people who may quit their jobs in a highly mobile workforce. However, general subsidies or training levies are not guaranteed to provide the skills that are most needed. Direct measurement of worker competences through literacy and life-skills surveys can give progressively better information about where the most important deficits lie. This reinforces the challenge to governments to structure support for job-related training in ways that are designed to enhance particular skills.

iv) An equitable distribution of investment

Greater equity of access and use of skills constitutes a major policy challenge.

The evidence shows that neither the stock of human capital nor the pattern of investment is well distributed among the adult workforce. There is a strong tendency for those with high knowledge, skills and competences to be those who acquire more, widening existing gaps. Considerations of equity in access to training and use of skills, not just in relation to initial education, but also in relation to the continuing investment in human capital over the life-cycle, are important. Labour market programmes targeted at the unemployed make a contribution. However, the distribution of other work-related training, whether sponsored by companies or by individuals, serves strongly to reinforce the inequalities created by initial education. An adult with tertiary education is more than twice as likely on average to participate in training during a twelve-month period than one who has not completed secondary school. While this is true within countries, however, it is significant that the least-educated adults in some countries train more frequently than the most-educated ones in others. So, low participation among the least-educated is not inevitable. In their partnerships with enterprises, governments will need to consider what instruments and incentives might help to achieve a better distribution.

v) Monitoring, measuring and accounting

The information base on human capital is inadequate not just from the point of view of policy makers but also in relation to the needs of private individuals and enterprises. Markets need good information to work well. Governments cannot exercise sole control over such information, but may be in a position to improve the available signals. One way might be to reform national accounting systems to reflect more accurately the importance and strategic role of human capital investments within "learning economies"; another is to encourage enterprises to revise their own accounting systems. If worker training were included as an investment rather than a current cost, and the competence of the workforce were reflected in companies' asset values, the incentive to invest would be changed.

There is considerable scope for building on what is known about human capital stocks, investments and returns. This may be achieved in particular, through developing indicators of where the most serious shortfalls in stock occur, and of the relationship between the cost of investing in these areas and the resulting benefits. The measures and monitoring should address the following framework of issues: levels of human capital investment; the nature of, and scope for co-investment; optimising the public outlays; and ensuring more equitable outcomes.

Better accounting for human capital as an investment can provide better signals to governments, businesses and individuals.

Annex

DATA FOR THE FIGURES

Table A2.1. **Two measures of educational attainment of the adult population**

Percentage of the population aged 25-64 by the highest completed level of education,
and estimated average number of years of schooling, 1995

(Data for Figure 2.1)

	Highest completed level of education		Average years of schooling
	Upper secondary or higher	Tertiary	
Australia	53	24	11.9
Austria	69	8	11.9
Belgium	53	25	11.7
Canada	75	47	13.2
Czech Republic	83	11	12.4
Denmark	62	20	12.4
Finland	65	21	11.6
France	68	19	11.2
Germany	84	23	13.4
Greece	43	17	10.9
Ireland	47	20	10.8
Italy	35	8	10.0
Netherlands	61	22	12.7
New Zealand	59	25	11.4
Norway	81	29	12.4
Portugal	20	11	10.0
Spain	28	16	11.2
Sweden	75	28	12.1
Switzerland	82	21	12.6
United Kingdom	76	21	12.1
United States	86	33	13.5
OECD average (unweighted)	62	21	11.9

Note: The estimates of average years of schooling relate to total cumulative duration of time spent in formal education over all ISCED levels from the beginning of primary level (ISCED 1) to tertiary level. These estimates are obtained by using data on educational attainment of each age-group from the Labour Force Survey and applying an estimated average cumulative duration for each level of education. Where there are programmes of different duration at the same ISCED level, a weighted average is taken based on weights corresponding to the number of persons in each broad educational programme.

Source: *Education at a Glance – OECD Indicators* (OECD, 1997b), indicator A2.1, p. 38 (using data on educational attainment of individuals from Labour Force Survey sources, or in the case of Denmark, *The Register of Educational Attainment of the Population*).

Table A2.2. **Percentage of younger (25-34 year olds) and older adults (45-54) with upper secondary education or higher, 1995**

(Data for Figure 2.2)

	25-34	45-54	Difference
Australia	57	51	6
Austria	81	66	17
Belgium	70	47	23
Canada	84	71	12
Czech Republic	91	83	11
Denmark	69	61	12
Finland	83	59	23
France	86	62	24
Germany	89	84	8
Greece	64	34	29
Ireland	64	36	22
Italy	49	28	19
Korea	86	39	39
Luxembourg	32	28	4
Netherlands	70	56	13
New Zealand	64	55	6
Norway	88	79	11
Poland	88	68	20
Portugal	31	16	14
Spain	47	18	26
Sweden	88	69	18
Switzerland	88	79	9
Turkey	26	20	6
United Kingdom	86	72	15
United States	87	86*	0
OECD average (unweighted)	71	55	15

*   Figure relates to 25-64 age-group.
Source: *Education at a Glance – OECD Indicators* (OECD, 1997b), indicator A2.2a, p. 39 (using data on educational attainment of individuals from Labour Force Survey sources, or in the case of Denmark, *The Register of Educational Attainment of the Population*).

Table A2.3. **Adults performing below an adequate threshold of literacy, 1994-95**

Percentage of population in various age-groups at literacy levels 1 or 2 on document scale

(Data for Figure 2.3)

	Age-group					
	16-65	Standard error	16-25	Standard error	46-55	Standard error
Australia	44.9	(0.4)	38.1	(1.1)	51.1	(1.3)
Belgium (Flanders)	39.6	(4.1)	23.6	(17.5)	48.3	(3.1)
Canada	42.9	(2.0)	32.6	(3.5)	54.0	(6.0)
Germany	41.7	(1.2)	34.2	(4.2)	42.4	(4.0)
Ireland	57.0	(2.3)	49.9	(2.7)	65.9	(3.1)
Netherlands	35.9	(0.7)	22.9	(2.4)	48.3	(2.6)
New Zealand	50.6	(0.9)	47.5	(2.0)	54.9	(2.6)
Poland	76.1	(0.7)	65.3	(2.2)	82.6	(2.5)
Sweden	25.1	(0.9)	19.7	(1.4)	26.6	(2.2)
Switzerland (French)	45.1	(1.3)	33.6	(3.1)	47.9	(4.0)
Switzerland (German)	47.2	(1.2)	32.8	(4.4)	54.8	(2.6)
United Kingdom	50.4	(1.0)	44.4	(2.5)	52.7	(2.4)
United States	49.6	(1.4)	55.5*	(3.3)	49.6	(2.9)

*   Because of a sampling anomaly, National Adult Literacy Survey data have been substituted for the group aged 16-25.
Source: International Adult Literacy Survey, 1994-95 (see also OECD, Human Resources Development Canada and Statistics Canada, 1997, *Literacy Skills for the Knowledge Society – Further Results from the International Adult Literacy Survey*, Paris).

Table A2.4. **Literacy levels of workers in different economic sectors**

Percentage of workers aged 16-65 with low (levels 1 or 2) and high (levels 4 or 5) literacy levels on document scale, 1994-95

(Data for Figure 2.4)

		Agriculture/ Mining	Standard error	Manufacturing	Standard error	Financial services	Standard error	Personal services	Standard error
Australia	Low	49.7	(2.9)	48.0	(1.8)	26.6	(1.7)	31.6	(1.1)
	High	13.2	(2.1)	16.9	(1.4)	27.0	(1.7)	27.4	(1.1)
Belgium (Flanders)	Low	56.1	(18.3)*	38.4	(3.7)	10.8	(3.5)*	23.1	(2.7)
	High	10.1	(12.4)*	16.5	(2.8)	36.0	(7.0)	24.5	(2.7)
Canada	Low	44.4	(8.1)	45.6	(5.1)	18.9	(9.1)	27.6	(6.0)
	High	22.7	(3.0)	23.2	(4.4)	47.4	(11.0)	32.0	(1.7)
Germany	Low	57.7	(9.6)*	35.0	(3.7)	25.4	(6.6)	28.5	(3.2)
	High	23.5	(9.4)*	21.5	(3.1)	21.9	(2.0)*	27.0	(2.9
Ireland	Low	65.3	(5.3)	50.7	(3.9)	34.4	(5.8)	38.9	(3.2)
	High	9.1	(3.1)*	12.9	(2.3)*	30.0	(7.2)	18.9	(2.1)
Netherlands	Low	29.7	(6.2)*	34.8	(3.3)	18.2	(2.8)	23.1	(1.2)
	High	22.1	(8.0)*	21.5	(2.8)	31.1	(2.7)	27.7	(1.6)
New Zealand	Low	56.1	(4.2)	57.5	(2.9)	29.6	(3.9)	36.2	(1.8)
	High	10.6	(2.1)	12.3	(1.9)	30.4	(3.6)	27.5	(1.9)
Poland	Low	86.9	(2.1)	78.3	(2.2)	52.7	(8.3)*	64.0	(2.4)
	High	2.3	(1.1)*	6.7	(1.1)*	17.9	(8.5)*	9.1	(1.2)
Sweden	Low	27.9	(6.1)*	21.7	(3.6)	13.2	(1.5)	22.5	(1.8)
	High	27.8	(8.2)*	38.6	(3.5)	52.3	(2.2)	36.1	(0.7)
Switzerland (French)	Low	63.2	(8.7)*	50.4	(5.1)	25.0	(5.5)*	34.5	(2.9)
	High	10.7	(4.6)*	11.0	(2.7)*	22.4	(4.5)*	22.0	(1.7)
Switzerland (German)	Low	60.6	(9.5)*	48.3	(5.4)	26.8	(5.6)	38.9	(3.4)
	High	7.9	(5.4)*	19.3	(4.6)	22.2	(3.2)	20.4	(2.0)
United Kingdom	Low	49.1	(6.5)	43.8	(2.1)	31.5	(3.6)	40.4	(2.3)
	High	12.1	(5.0)*	21.8	(2.0)	35.3	(3.7)	24.8	(1.8)
United States	Low	42.0	(11.7)*	53.3	(3.9)	37.1	(4.6)	35.0	(1.8)
	High	32.0	(9.5)*	16.2	(2.1)	27.4	(3.1)	26.8	(2.1)

* Sample size is insufficient to permit a reliable estimate.

Source: International Adult Literacy Survey, 1994-95 (see also OECD, Human Resources Development Canada and Statistics Canada, 1997, *Literacy Skills for the Knowledge Society – Further Results from the International Adult Literacy Survey*, Paris).

Table A2.5. **Adult literacy and educational attainment**

Mean document scores for persons aged 16-65, on a scale with a range of 500 points, by level of educational attainment, 1994-95

(Data for Figure 2.5)

	Less than upper secondary		Upper secondary only		Tertiary		All levels	
	Mean	Standard error	Mean	Standard error	Mean	Standard error	Mean	Standard error
Australia	243.5	(1.7)	287.9	(1.7)	293.1	(1.1)	273.3	(1.0)
Belgium (Flanders)	250.9	(5.3)	288.6	(2.1)	313.3	(1.5)	278.2	(3.2)
Canada	227.1	(5.7)	288.0	(5.3)	318.4	(4.9)	279.3	(3.0)
Germany	276.1	(1.1)	295.4	(2.2)	314.5	(1.6)	285.1	(1.0)
Ireland	231.5	(2.6)	280.5	(2.9)	303.5	(3.3)	259.2	(3.2)
Netherlands	262.6	(1.5)	302.3	(1.4)	311.2	(1.6)	286.9	(0.9)
New Zealand	244.5	(2.3)	287.3	(2.0)	302.1	(1.5)	269.1	(1.3)
Poland	201.5	(1.7)	251.5	(2.0)	275.6	(3.9)	223.9	(1.8)
Sweden	280.6	(2.4)	308.3	(1.0)	331.2	(2.0)	305.6	(0.9)
Switzerland (French)	235.0	(4.1)	283.4	(2.2)	312.5	(2.7)	274.1	(1.7)
Switzerland (German)	230.6	(6.2)	283.2	(2.1)	300.4	(2.7)	269.7	(2.0)
United Kingdom	247.4	(2.4)	285.5	(3.1)	311.8	(1.9)	267.5	(1.9)
United States	199.9	(4.6)	266.1	(2.3)	302.5	(2.4)	267.9	(1.7)

Source: International Adult Literacy Survey, 1994-95 (see pages 150 and 152 in OECD, Human Resources Development Canada and Statistics Canada, 1997, *Literacy Skills for the Knowledge Society – Further Results from the International Adult Literacy Survey*, Paris).

Table A2.6. **Difference in educational attainment between men and women aged 25-64**

Comparing the difference in percentage-point terms for men and women, 1995

	Men	Women	Difference
Australia	64	42	22
Austria	76	62	14
Belgium	55	53	2
Canada	74	76	-2
Czech Republic	90	77	13
Denmark	66	58	8
Finland	64	67	-3
France	73	64	9
Germany	89	78	11
Greece	45	40	5
Ireland	43	51	-8
Italy	37	33	4
Korea	70	50	20
Luxembourg	34	25	9
Netherlands	67	56	11
New Zealand	64	55	9
Norway	82	81	1
Poland	76	71	5
Portugal	20	20	0
Spain	31	26	5
Sweden	73	77	-4
Switzerland	88	76	12
Turkey	26	20	6
United Kingdom	81	70	11
United States	85	87	-2
OECD average (unweighted)	63	57	6

Source: OECD education database (using data on educational attainment of individuals from Labour Force Survey or, in the case of Denmark, *The Register of Educational Attainment of the Population*).

Table A2.7. **The intergenerational educational gap**

Countries ranked by magnitude of intergenerational educational gap		Evolution of gap from older to younger generation	Tertiary offsprings/ Parents with less than upper secondary education	Tertiary offsprings/ Parents with tertiary education
Australia	1.96	Increasing	More inequality	No change
New Zealand	2.11	Increasing	More inequality	More inequality
Sweden	2.15	Increasing	More inequality	Less inequality
Canada	2.41	Increasing	More inequality	No change
United Kingdom	2.85	Increasing	More inequality	Less inequality
Belgium (Flanders)	3.25	Narrowing	More inequality	Less inequality
United States	3.27	Narrowing	No change	Less inequality
Netherlands	3.33	Narrowing	No change	Less inequality
Switzerland	4.28	Narrowing	No change	No change
Ireland	4.77	–	–	–
Poland	5.84	–	More inequality	–

Note: Older age-group represents persons aged 46-55, younger age-group represents persons aged 26-35. The above table shows the ratio of the probability of reaching tertiary level attainment for individuals whose parents have also completed some form of tertiary level education relative to the probability of attaining tertiary education for individuals whose parents have not completed secondary school. This ratio is referred to as the "Intergenerational Educational Gap".

Source: Data are from IALS and analysis was undertaken by de Broucker, P. and Underwood, K. (1997), "An indicator of equity: The probability of attaining a post-secondary credential by the level of parents' education", Working Paper for Network B of the OECD INES project, Centre for Education Statistics, Statistics Canada, Ottawa.

Table A3.1. **Spending on education, research and development relative
to national income, 1994**

(Data for Figure 3.1)

Total expenditure relative to GDP and annual spending per student relative
to per capita GDP

	Spending on formal education					Spending on research and development[4] (including spending in tertiary education)
	Public and private[1]	Public sources only[2]	Total annual spending per student as a percentage of GDP per capita[3]			
	Percentage of GDP		Primary	Secondary	Tertiary	
Australia	6.2	4.8	16	26	52	1.6
Austria	5.6	5.4	27	35	43	1.6
Belgium	–	5.5	16	28	31	1.6
Canada	7.2	6.7	–	–	56	1.6
Czech Republic	–	5.7	20	30	60	1.3
Denmark	8.4	6.6	24	31	42	1.9
Finland	8.0	6.6	24	28	37	2.3
France	6.7	5.6	17	30	31	2.4
Germany	6.0	4.5	17	31	43	2.3
Greece	–	3.1	–	13	23	0.5
Hungary	6.5	5.7	27	27	81	0.9
Ireland	6.0	5.2	13	22	48	1.4
Italy	4.8	4.7	24	28	26	1.2
Japan	4.9	3.8	19	22	42	2.6
Korea	6.2	3.7	18	21	44	2.7
Mexico	5.9	4.5	13	25	74	0.3
Netherlands	6.0	4.7	16	22	46	2.0
New Zealand	–	6.0	16	27	50	1.0
Norway	–	6.8	–	–	–	1.7
Portugal	5.7	5.3	–	–	–	0.6
Spain	6.4	4.8	19	24	30	0.9
Sweden	9.0	6.6	29	31	73	3.6
Switzerland	–	5.6	25	30	66	–
Turkey	4.2	3.4	13	10	66	0.4
United Kingdom	–	4.9	19	25	43	2.1
United States	6.8	4.9	21	26	61	2.5
OECD average (unweighted)	6.3	5.2	20	26	49	1.6

– Missing data.
1. Total expenditure from public, private and international sources for education (including payments for student living costs and educational materials).
2. Total public expenditure for educational institutions (excluding public subsidies for student living costs).
3. Data refer to expenditure for both public and private institutions with the exception of:
   – Austria, the Czech Republic, Germany, Hungary, Italy, Norway, Switzerland, Turkey where only public institutions were included;
   – Belgium, Greece and the United Kingdom for which independent private institutions were excluded.
4. Spending on research and development refer to 1995 data in the case of Denmark, Korea, New Zealand, Norway, Portugal and Sweden and 1993 data in the case of Greece.
Sources: For education spending, see *Education at a Glance – OECD Indicators* (OECD, 1997c), indicator B1.1a, p. 62 and indicator B4.2, p. 102; for research and development spending, Main Science Technology Indicators Database (DSTI/OECD), November 1997.

Table A3.2. **Average expected years of formal education, 1995**

(Data for Figure 3.2)

A. Estimated average number of years in formal education for a 5-year-old child if 1995 enrolment patterns prevailed in the future

B. Estimated average number of years in tertiary education for a 17-year-old if 1995 tertiary enrolment patterns prevailed in the future

	5-year-old child (all levels) A	17-year-old (tertiary education) B
Australia	16.3	3.0
Austria	15.2	1.8
Belgium	17.6	2.5
Canada	16.0	3.7
Czech Republic	14.1	1.1
Denmark	16.3	2.1
Finland	15.9	2.8
France	16.3	2.5
Germany	16.2	1.8
Greece	14.0	1.9
Hungary	14.2	1.1
Ireland	15.2	2.1
Korea	14.1	2.6
Mexico	11.7	0.8
Netherlands	16.9	2.1
New Zealand	16.0	2.5
Norway	16.2	2.4
Portugal	15.7	1.8
Spain	16.1	2.3
Sweden	15.8	1.8
Switzerland	15.4	1.4
Turkey	9.3	1.0
United Kingdom	15.3	2.0
United States	15.8	3.3
OECD average	15.2	2.1

Source: Education at a Glance – OECD Indicators (OECD, 1997c), indicator C1.2, p. 141 and indicator C5.1, p. 170.

Table A3.3. **Percentage participation by employed adults (aged 25-64) in job-related training, 1994-95**

(Data for Figure 3.3)

	International Adult Literacy Survey, 1994[1] (standard errors in parentheses)	Labour Force and other Household Surveys (various years)[2]		European Labour Force Survey, 1995[3]
Reference period:	12 months	12 months	Year of survey	4 weeks
Australia	38.1 (0.6)	38	1995	–
Austria	–	–	–	7.3
Belgium[4]	20.0 (1.4)	–	–	2.4
Canada	37.5 (2.7)	28	1993	–
Denmark	–	–	–	15.8
Finland	–	45	1995	4.5
France	–	40	1994	0.5[5]
Germany[6]	–	33	1994	3.9
Greece	–	–	–	0.5
Ireland	23.4 (2.4)	–	–	4.8
Italy	–	–	–	1.1
Luxembourg	–	–	–	2.2
Netherlands	32.5 (1.3)	–	–	14.1[5]
New Zealand	46.9 (1.5)	–	–	–
Poland	16.5 (1.2)	–	–	–
Portugal	–	–	–	2.0[5]
Spain	–	–	–	1.1
Sweden[7]	–	42	1996	15.9
Switzerland[8]	31.7 (1.3)	35	1996	–
United Kingdom	51.9 (1.4)	–	–	12.4
United States	45.6 (1.5)	34	1995	–

– Missing data.

Job-related training refers to all courses undertaken for career or job-related purposes as distinct from personal or other interests.

1. The data derived from IALS refer to job-training in the previous 12 months. Job-related training refers to all courses, workshops, on-the-job training or apprenticeship training undertaken for career or job-related purposes as distinct from personal or other interests.
2. Data taken from European and other LFS sources include all types of organised job-related training except for full-time studies at tertiary level. The USA data are from the National Household Education Survey, 1995. Data for Canada are from the Adult Education and Training Survey. Data for France are taken from both an administrative enterprise source (Ministry of Labour) as well as the *Labour Force Survey*.
3. The data derived from the European *Labour Force Survey* refer to vocational training in the previous 4 weeks.
4. Belgium Flanders (IALS data only).
5. Data on training from the European *Labour Force Survey* in relation to France, Netherlands and Portugal relate to current participation by adults in job-related training as distinct from training over the previous 4 weeks.
6. Data from IALS for Germany are not included in the above table because the question on training in the IALS background questionnaire related to continuing vocational training rather than adult education defined more broadly.
7. Data from the *Labour Force Survey* in Sweden relate to a six-month period and include only training paid for, or sponsored by the employer.
8. Result from IALS relates to French and German-speaking parts of Switzerland combined (but excluding Italian-speaking community which was not part of the first round of IALS in 1994-95).

Sources: Special tabulations from the International Adult Literacy Survey, 1994-95 (see OECD, Human Resources Development Canada and Statistics Canada, 1997, *Literacy Skills for the Knowledge Society – Further Results from the International Adult Literacy Survey*, Paris); *Education at a Glance – OECD Indicators* (OECD, 1996b), indicator P8, p. 131 and *Education at a Glance – OECD Indicators* (OECD, 1997c), indicator C7.1a, p. 195; European Labour Force Survey (1995).

Table A3.4. **Average duration[1] of job-related training[2] undertaken by employed adults aged 25-64, 1994-95**

(Data for Figure 3.4)

	Rate of participation in job-related training (% of all employed)	Average duration in hours per *person trained*	Average duration in hours per *person employed*[3]
	Standard errors in parentheses		
	[1]	[2]	[3] = [2] × [1]/100
Australia	38.1 (0.6)	115.9 (9.0)	44.2
Belgium (Flanders)	20.0 (1.4)	126.2 (17.7)	25.2
Canada	37.5 (2.7)	119.8 (7.1)	44.9
Ireland	23.4 (2.4)	218.7 (26.9)	51.2
Netherlands	32.5 (1.3)	159.0 (14.9)	51.7
New Zealand	46.9 (1.5)	154.1 (12.1)	72.2
Poland	16.5 (1.2)	143.2 (17.2)	23.6
Switzerland[4]	31.7 (1.3)	114.1 (8.8)	36.2
United Kingdom	51.9 (1.4)	99.5 (4.8)	51.6
United States	45.6 (1.5)	98.1 (9.4)	44.6
Average (unweighted)	34.4	134.9	46.4

1. The average duration of job-related training is the total average amount in hours over the previous 12 months in respect of the three most important mentions of such training by respondents in the *International Adult Literacy Survey.*
2. Data on duration of job-related training were not available in the case of Sweden.
3. The average duration in hours of job-related training per person employed in column 3 is the total number of hours of such training divided by the total number of employed persons aged 25-64.
4. See notes to Table A3.3 above.
Source: Special tabulations from the International Adult Literacy Survey, 1994-95 (see OECD, Human Resources Development Canada and Statistics Canada, 1997, *Literacy Skills for the Knowledge Society – Further Results from the International Adult Literacy Survey*, Paris).

Table A3.5. **Participation by adults aged 25-64 in continuing education
and training by type of training (job-related or other)
and by labour force status, 1994-95**

		Employed	Unemployed	Inactive
		Standard errors in parentheses		
Australia	All types of training	42.2 (0.6)	28.3 (3.1)	16.1 (1.0)
	Job related	38.1 (0.6)	23.8 (3.0)	6.9 (0.8)
	Other	4.1 (0.3)	4.5* (1.4)	9.2 (0.9)
Belgium (Flanders)	All types of training	27.0 (1.4)	16.6* (3.8)	9.8 (1.7)
	Job related	20.0 (1.4)	8.6* (2.5)	0.9* (0.4)
	Other	7.0 (0.8)	8.0* (2.8)	8.9 (1.7)
Canada	All types of training	41.9 (3.3)	30.1 (8.5)	23.1 (4.4)
	Job related	37.5 (2.7)	22.0 (6.8)	9.9 (3.6)
	Other	4.5 (1.5)	8.1* (4.9)	13.2 (1.5)
Ireland	All types of training	29.5 (3.2)	8.5* (3.4)	14.5 (2.4)
	Job related	23.4 (2.4)	7.1* (2.8)	6.6 (1.6)
	Other	6.1 (1.2)	1.5* (1.0)	7.9 (1.3)
Netherlands	All types of training	43.2 (1.1)	39.2 (4.6)	21.8 (1.7)
	Job related	32.5 (1.3)	29.7 (4.4)	5.9 (1.0)
	Other	10.7 (0.8)	9.5* (2.8)	15.9 (1.4)
New Zealand	All types of training	53.1 (1.6)	31.4 (3.8)	29.7 (2.5)
	Job related	46.9 (1.5)	24.1 (4.2)	16.3 (2.0)
	Other	6.2 (0.7)	7.3 (3.4)	13.4 (1.9)
Poland	All types of training	20.5 (1.4)	7.9* (2.0)	2.8* (0.6)
	Job related	16.5 (1.2)	2.4* (1.5)	1.1* (0.3)
	Other	4.0 (0.7)	5.5* (1.5)	1.7* (0.4)
Sweden	All types of training	60.2 (1.0)	46.0 (4.0)	28.9 (2.4)
	Job related	–	–	–
	Other	–	–	–
Switzerland[1]	All types of training	45.7 (1.3)	32.2* (7.3)	27.8 (2.4)
	Job related	31.7 (1.3)	27.0* (9.1)	6.0 (1.2)
	Other	14.0 (1.2)	5.2* (3.4)	21.8 (2.4)
United Kingdom	All types of training	56.0 (1.1)	33.1 (3.2)	14.3 (1.8)
	Job related	51.9 (1.4)	24.0 (2.9)	7.0 (1.3)
	Other	4.1 (0.7)	9.0 (1.9)	7.3 (1.3)
United States	All types of training	49.0 (1.5)	30.2* (4.5)	17.1 (2.1)
	Job related	45.6 (1.5)	28.5* (4.4)	10.1 (1.8)
	Other	3.5 (0.5)	1.7* (1.4)	7.0 (1.4)
Average	All types of training[2]	42.6	27.6	18.7
(unweighted)	Job related	34.4	19.7	7.1
	Other	6.4	6.0	10.6

Note: This table shows the percentage of each group (employed, unemployed, inactive) who received training in the previous 12 months. See notes to Table A3.3 for definitions of training.
* Indicates less than 30 cases in the sample cell.
1. See notes to Table A3.3 above.
2. Average participation rate for all types of training includes those for Sweden. However, Sweden is not included in the averages for job-related and other training. Hence, the sum of the averages for the latter two types of training does not equal the average on all types of training.
Source: Special tabulations from the International Adult Literacy Survey, 1994-95 (see OECD, Human Resources Development Canada and Statistics Canada, 1997, *Literacy Skills for the Knowledge Society – Further Results from the International Adult Literacy Survey*, Paris).

Table A3.6. **Participation by employed adults aged 25-64 in job-related training by level of education, 1994-95**

	Below upper secondary	Upper secondary	Tertiary	All
	Standard errors in parentheses			
Australia	26.2 (1.1)	36.4 (1.3)	53.4 (1.3)	38.1 (0.6)
Belgium (Flanders)	7.4* (2.0)	20.2 (2.5)	32.7 (2.0)	20.0 (1.4)
Canada	20.8 (5.1)	28.9 (3.3)	52.7 (5.4)	37.5 (2.7)
Ireland	14.8 (3.0)	24.1 (2.7)	37.8 (3.3)	23.4 (2.4)
Netherlands	20.9 (2.1)	34.5 (2.1)	45.5 (2.4)	32.5 (1.3)
New Zealand	37.0 (2.9)	46.7 (2.6)	62.3 (2.5)	46.9 (1.5)
Poland	8.0 (0.8)	25.0 (3.3)	29.1 (2.0)	16.5 (1.2)
Switzerland	9.0* (2.9)	34.4 (2.0)	43.8 (3.0)	31.7 (1.3)
United Kingdom	40.8 (1.8)	55.4 (4.8)	73.2 (1.7)	51.9 (1.4)
United States	17.4 (3.1)	34.4 (2.2)	63.1 (2.3)	45.6 (1.5)
Average (unweighted)	20.2	34.0	49.4	34.4

*   Indicates less than 30 cases in the sample cell.
Source: Special tabulations from the International Adult Literacy Survey, 1994-95 (see OECD, Human Resources Development Canada and Statistics Canada, 1997, *Literacy Skills for the Knowledge Society – Further Results from the International Adult Literacy Survey*, Paris).

Table A3.7. **Participation by employed adults aged 25-64 in job-related training, by age-group, 1994-95**

	Age-group			
	25-34	35-44	45-64	All
	Standard errors in parentheses			
Australia	42.9 (1.3)	41.7 (1.3)	30.7 (1.2)	38.1 (0.6)
Belgium (Flanders)	21.4 (2.1)	17.0 (1.6)	21.6 (2.8)	20.0 (1.4)
Canada	41.4 (5.0)	39.7 (3.1)	31.6 (5.4)	37.5 (2.7)
Ireland	27.5 (2.9)	23.6 (2.9)	18.8 (3.3)	23.4 (2.4)
Netherlands	36.3 (2.0)	35.5 (2.3)	25.2 (2.1)	32.5 (1.3)
New Zealand	50.2 (2.4)	49.4 (1.9)	41.9 (3.2)	46.9 (1.5)
Poland	17.0 (1.7)	17.6 (1.9)	14.4 (1.5)	16.5 (1.2)
Switzerland[1]	35.5 (2.7)	32.1 (2.6)	28.2 (1.8)	31.7 (1.3)
United Kingdom	59.1 (2.2)	58.0 (2.1)	41.3 (1.9)	51.9 (1.4)
United States	46.2 (3.3)	48.1 (2.0)	43.3 (2.0)	45.6 (1.5)
Average (unweighted)	37.7	36.3	29.7	34.4

1.   See notes to Table A3.3 above.
Source: Special tabulations from the International Adult Literacy Survey, 1994-95 (see OECD, Human Resources Development Canada and Statistics Canada, 1997, *Literacy Skills for the Knowledge Society – Further Results from the International Adult Literacy Survey*, Paris).

Table A4.1a. **Percentage of women aged 30-44 in employment, by level of educational attainment, 1995**

(Data for Figure 4.1A)

	Below upper secondary	Upper-secondary only	Tertiary non-university	Tertiary university	Total
Australia	60	66	76	83	66
Austria	63	75	89	88	73
Belgium	48	70	87	83	66
Canada	51	70	77	82	71
Czech Republic	78	89	–	95	87
Denmark	69	84	91	93	79
Finland	62	73	82	86	73
France	53	71	84	79	69
Germany	56	70	83	82	69
Greece	44	51	73	86	54
Ireland	31	55	75	81	50
Italy	38	66	–	81	52
Korea	67	49	–	49	56
Luxembourg	48	69	–	79	55
Netherlands	47	66	–	81	63
New Zealand	60	69	74	77	67
Norway	59	79	84	90	79
Poland	59	70	86	92	72
Portugal	67	80	94	95	73
Spain	33	51	55	77	43
Sweden	70	83	90	89	83
Switzerland	69	69	73	78	70
Turkey	31	33	–	67	33
United Kingdom	51	70	84	84	69
United States	49	72	82	81	73
OECD average (unweighted)	55	68	81	82	66

–   Missing values or category not applicable.

Source: *Education Policy Analysis* (OECD, 1997*b*), p. 101; and *Education at a Glance – OECD Indicators* (OECD, 1997*a*), indicator E2.1b, p. 252 (using data on educational attainment of individuals from Labour Force Survey data or, in the case of Denmark, *The Register of Educational Attainment of the Population*).

Table A4.1b. **Expected years of unemployment over a working lifetime by level of educational attainment for men aged 25-64, 1995**

(Data for Figure 4.1B)

Based on unemployment-to-population ratios for different age-groups

	Below upper secondary	Upper secondary only	Tertiary	All levels combined	Difference in years between tertiary and below upper secondary
Australia	3.5	2.2	1.6	2.5	2.0
Austria	1.6	0.9	0.6	1.0	1.0
Belgium	3.0	1.4	0.9	2.0	2.1
Canada	4.1	2.8	2.3	2.8	1.8
Czech Republic	2.8	0.6	0.2	0.7	2.6
Denmark	4.0	2.8	2.0	3.1	2.0
Finland	6.8	5.8	3.1	5.3	3.7
France	4.4	2.5	2.1	2.8	2.3
Germany	4.5	2.3	1.6	2.4	2.9
Greece	1.8	1.7	1.9	1.8	−0.1
Ireland	5.0	2.3	1.4	3.5	3.6
Italy	2.2	1.4	1.8	1.9	0.4
Korea	0.6	0.6	0.6	0.6	0.0
Luxembourg	0.7	0.6	0.1	0.6	0.6
Netherlands	1.9	1.1	1.1	1.4	0.8
New Zealand	2.3	1.1	1.2	1.5	1.1
Norway	2.2	1.4	0.9	1.4	1.2
Poland	4.6	2.9	1.3	3.0	3.4
Portugal	1.9	1.6	1.4	1.8	0.5
Spain	5.6	3.9	2.9	4.8	2.6
Sweden	4.3	3.3	2.0	3.2	2.4
Switzerland	2.3	0.9	0.7	1.0	1.6
Turkey	1.7	1.6	1.0	1.6	0.8
United Kingdom	5.4	2.9	1.6	3.0	3.8
United States	3.0	1.7	1.1	1.7	2.0
OECD average (unweighted)	3.2	2.0	1.4	2.2	1.8

Note: Expected years of unemployment represent the average number of years an individual would spend in unemployment over a working lifetime for a given level of educational attainment at current rates of unemployment. It is estimated by summing across age-bands, the value of unemployment-to-population ratios multiplied by the number of years in each band: $E = \Sigma\ u_{ij}\ {}^*L/POP_{ij}$ where u_{ij} = the total number of persons who are unemployed at age-group i and level of educational attainment j, POP_{ij} = the total number of persons at age-group i and level of educational attainment j, and L = number of years in the age-band (usually 5 since age-bands are defined as 15-19, 20-24 etc.). The measure takes no account of the impact of the economic cycle on unemployment or the possibility of widening unemployment rates across educational levels over time.

Source: Education at a Glance – OECD Indicators (OECD, 1997a), indicator A3.1a, p. 46 (using data on educational attainment of individuals from Labour Force Survey data or, in the case of Denmark, The Register of Educational Attainment of the Population).

Table A4.2a. **Education and earnings of women aged 30-44, 1995**

(Data for Figure 4.2A)

Mean earnings relative to upper secondary level only (100)

	Below upper secondary	Non-university tertiary	University tertiary
Australia	86	102	144
Canada	–	114	167
Czech Republic	77	–	154
Denmark	86	108	129
Finland	91	123	169
France	73	139	170
Germany	88	114	165
Ireland[1]	61	123	197
Italy	76	–	120
Netherlands	71	134	160
New Zealand	84	108	146
Norway	80	131	147
Portugal	63	–	174
Sweden	86	111	138
Switzerland	76	145	161
United Kingdom	76	159	210
United States	59	127	186
OECD average (unweighted)	77	124	161

–   Missing values or category not applicable.
1.   Data refer to 1994.
Source: Education Policy Analysis (OECD, 1997b), pp. 33 and 102, and *Education at a Glance – OECD Indicators*
            (OECD, 1997a), indicator E4.1b, p. 266 (using data from various national household and labour force
            surveys or income registers – for further details see OECD, 1997a, p. 382).

Table A4.2b. **Education and earnings of men aged 30-44, 1995**

(Data for Figure 4.2B)

Mean earnings relative to upper secondary level only (100)

	Below upper secondary	Non-university tertiary	University tertiary
Australia	101	118	163
Canada	82	110	150
Czech Republic	71	–	154
Denmark	87	107	138
Finland	89	121	175
France	86	138	180
Germany	90	105	148
Ireland[1]	78	122	169
Italy	79	–	139
Netherlands	83	121	148
New Zealand	82	102	163
Norway	81	129	153
Portugal	62	–	176
Sweden	88	119	152
Switzerland	74	122	132
United Kingdom	77	115	162
United States	63	120	170
OECD average (unweighted)	81	118	157

–   Missing values or category not applicable.
1.   Data refer to 1994.
Source: Education Policy Analysis (OECD,1997b), pp. 33 and 102, and *Education at a Glance – OECD Indicators*
            (OECD, 1997a), indicator E4.1b, p. 266 (using data from various national Household and Labour Force
            Surveys or Income registers – for further details see OECD, 1997a, p. 382).

Table A4.3. **Estimates of private, fiscal and social rates of return to education at university tertiary level for men and women, 1995**

Note that the data presented in this table are based on model of simulated private and fiscal benefits at tertiary level education. They are illustrative of on-going developmental work and should therefore be treated with caution

	Men			Women		
	Private[1]	Fiscal[2]	"Social"[3]	Private	Fiscal	"Social"
Australia	14	10	11	21	10	13
Belgium	14	9	9	8	13	9
Canada	14	7	9	21	7	11
Denmark	8	8	8	7	8	8
France	20	11	13	28	9	13
Sweden	–	6	9	–	4	7
United States	11	9	10	12	9	11

– Missing value or category not applicable.
1. Private returns are estimated on the basis of additional income of individuals for a given level of education over a working lifetime (to the age 64), including social transfers and non-labour income, and after deduction of income taxes and employee social security contributions, compared with additional private costs of tuition and forgone earnings for a given level of education.
2. Fiscal returns were based on the estimated value of additional income tax receipts and employee social security contributions less social transfers over a lifetime compared with the public costs of tuition and taxes on forgone earnings for a given level of education.
3. "Social" rates of returns are, thus a combination (or weighted average) of private and fiscal returns, but they exclude externalities or "spill-over" effects.
Source: OECD INES Network B Pilot Survey of private, fiscal and social returns to education (forthcoming working paper in 1998).

Table A4.4. **Annual rates of return to education**

(Data for Figure 4.4)

Estimated at different levels over a working lifetime in respect of employed persons only, 1995

	Women			Men			Rate of return on business capital[1]
	Upper secondary education	Non-university tertiary	University education	Upper secondary education	Non-university tertiary	University education	
Australia	12.5	7.9	6.7	7.5	9.7	10.4	13.6
Canada	16.1	28.1	28.5	12.5	23.0	16.5	19.3
Czech Republic	13.8	–	7.0	22.0	–	8.7	–
Denmark	11.8	5.1	9.2	10.4	5.2	11.0	10.7
Finland	8.1	12.2	14.3	10.4	10.5	14.8	9.4
France	14.1	20.1	12.7	14.2	17.6	14.1	15.0
Germany	5.5	8.7	8.2	5.7	16.6	10.9	13.7
Ireland[2]	28.8	8.2	17.4	18.6	11.7	14.0	14.4
Italy	9.5	–	4.6	10.4	–	9.9	15.9
Netherlands	24.4	–	10.5	14.1	–	10.8	17.9
New Zealand	11.2	–0.5	10.3	12.8	–11.5	11.6	18.5
Norway	17.3	7.8	13.3	11.3	9.4	11.6	7.6
Portugal	32.4	–	28.3	33.3	–	27.3	–
Sweden	9.9	4.2	5.3	10.9	6.5	8.2	14.2
Switzerland	22.1	17.7	5.2	19.0	27.1	5.5	4.2
United Kingdom	19.1	13.7	19.1	14.3	4.8	12.7	11.8
United States	22.9	10.5	12.6	26.3	8.9	12.6	18.3
Average (unweighted)	16.4	11.1	12.5	14.9	10.7	12.4	13.6
Coefficient of variation for above[3]	0.44	0.68	0.56	0.46	0.89	0.36	0.30

Note:

The estimates in this table are internal rates of return estimated by finding the rate of discount that equates *i)* the present value of an estimated future stream of additional gross earnings over a lifetime (from age 16-64) as a result of more education, to *ii)* the present value of the total cost of graduating at a higher level of education (including forgone earnings). No account is taken of the risk of unemployment over a working lifetime, as the calculation relates to persons in employment only. It is assumed that annual average earnings grow over time at a uniform rate of 1 per cent for all individuals regardless of educational attainment level. Formally, this calculation consists of estimating, for educational attainment level i, the rate of interest (r) that equates the present value of a stream of additional earnings $(E_i - E_{i-1})$ over a working lifetime with the discounted additional costs $(C_i - C_{i-1})$ of producing a graduate at ISCED level i compared to level i – 1: $\Sigma(E_{i,t} - E_{i-1,t})/(1 + r)^t = \Sigma(C_{i,t} - C_{i-1,t})/(1 + r)^t$

The value of t is the time at which each observation of earnings or cost is estimated. On the earnings side, t relates to the working lifetime following exit from schooling. On the cost side, t refers to the duration of a given level of education. Refer to Alsalam, N. and Conley, R. (1995), "The rate of return to education: a proposal for an indicator", *Education and Employment*, Centre for Educational Research and Innovation, OECD, Paris.

*   Missing value or category not applicable.
.   Data on rates of return to business capital (including housing) were obtained from *OECD Economic Outlook*, No. 61, June 1997, Annex Table 25.
2. Data refer to 1994.
3. Ratio of the standard deviation to the average.

Source: *Education Policy Analysis* (OECD, 1997*b*), pp. 35 and 102, and *Education at a Glance – OECD Indicators* (OECD, 1997*a*), indicator E5.1, p. 272.

OECD PUBLICATIONS, 2, rue André-Pascal, 75775 PARIS CEDEX 16
PRINTED IN FRANCE
(96 98 02 1 P) ISBN 92-64-16067-1 – No. 50053 1998